Tennessee's

Forests, 2004

Christopher M. Oswalt, Sonja N. Oswalt,
Tony G. Johnson, James L. Chamberlain,
KaDonna C. Randolph, and John W. Coulston

United States
Department of
Agriculture

Forest Service

Southern
Research Station

Resource Bulletin
SRS–144

Author Contributions

Christopher M. Oswalt contributed the outline of the report; initial analyses; and all text, tables, and figures not attributed to coauthors or acknowledged otherwise. Chris was also responsible for compiling coauthor contributions, the majority of the photographs, and completing two revisions of the report following peer-review.

Sonja N. Oswalt contributed the text, tables, and figures for the "Deadwood in," Tennessee Forest Land," and "Invasive Plant Species" sections.

Tony G. Johnson contributed text, tables, and figures for the "Timber Products and the Economy" and "Timber Products Output and Removals" sections.

James L. Chamberlain contributed text, tables, and figures for the "Nontimber Forest Products" section.

KaDonna C. Randolph contributed text and tables for the "Tree Crown Health" section.

John W. Coulston contributed the analysis and figures for the regional and national ozone figures, and the analyses and map in the "Fragmentation" section.

Christopher M. Oswalt is a Forester with the U.S. Department of Agriculture Forest Service, Southern Research Station, Forest Inventory and Analysis Research Work Unit, Knoxville, TN 37919.

Sonja N. Oswalt is a Forester with the U.S. Department of Agriculture Forest Service, Southern Research Station, Forest Inventory and Analysis Research Work Unit, Knoxville, TN 37919.

Tony G. Johnson is a Supervisory Forester with the U.S. Department of Agriculture Forest Service, Southern Research Station, Forest Inventory and Analysis Research Work Unit, Knoxville, TN 37919.

James L. Chamberlain is a Research Forest Products Technologist with the U.S. Department of Agriculture Forest Service, Southern Research Station, Forest Products Conservation Work Unit, Blacksburg, VA 24060.

KaDonna C. Randolph is a Mathematical Statistician with the U.S. Department of Agriculture Forest Service, Southern Research Station, Forest Inventory and Analysis Research Work Unit, Knoxville, TN 37919.

John W. Coulston is a Supervisory Research Forester with the U.S. Department of Agriculture Forest Service, Southern Research Station, Forest Inventory and Analysis Research Work Unit, Knoxville, TN 37919.

All photographs taken by Christopher M. Oswalt unless otherwise noted.

Front cover: top left, mixed hardwood forests along the banks of the Tennessee River; top right, mature hardwood forest in west Tennessee; bottom, yellow trillium (*Trillium luteum*). Back cover: top left, Cherokee National Forest; top right, mixed hardwood forests along the banks of the Tennessee River; bottom, *Sassafras albidum* is one of many hardwood tree species that are found growing in Tennessee forests.

Mountain laurel (*Kalmia latifolia*).

Tennessee's

Forests, 2004

Christopher M. Oswalt, Sonja N. Oswalt,
Tony G. Johnson, James L. Chamberlain,
KaDonna C. Randolph, and John W. Coulston

A Table Mountain pine
(*Pinus pungens*) stand on the
Cherokee National Forest in
east Tennessee.

Steve G. Scott

Jimmy L. Reaves

The State of Tennessee celebrates a rich history rooted in its natural environment and a forest resource that is diverse and productive. The citizens of Tennessee receive multiple benefits from an extensive forest resource in the State, including timber and nontimber forest products, recreational opportunities (e.g., hiking, hunting, and camping), and clean water and air. With so much at stake and because the general public, policy makers, and resource managers need information that documents changes taking place in our forests, it is important to have the best available means for assessing the extent and condition of our forest resources.

Since the 1930s, the Forest Service, U.S. Department of Agriculture, has provided these means through the Forest Inventory and Analysis (FIA) Program, which conducts inventories of public and private lands, Nationwide, at regular time intervals. Over the past 10 years, FIA has approached this inventory work in an exciting new manner by forming partnerships with State Forestry organizations. The working partnership between the Tennessee Department of Agriculture, Division of Forestry, and the Forest Service, Southern Research Station, FIA Program has improved and strengthened Tennessee's forest inventory. The quality of this report is a direct result of that sustained cooperation.

This report contains information on the forest lands of Tennessee that is used by policy makers, agency and organization leaders, resource managers and owners, researchers, and students involved in forest resource management and forest-related issues. Because forests are much more than just tree volume and numbers of trees, this report includes information on forest health, ecological values, socio-economic benefits, and biological diversity and includes an evaluation of a survey concerning the goals and objectives of Tennessee forest landowners.

It is with great pride that we present this information about the forests of Tennessee. It is our goal that the partnership between our two organizations and the cooperative nature of this effort will continue to deliver the best information on the forests of Tennessee now and in the future.

Steve G. Scott
Tennessee State Forester
Tennessee Division of Forestry

Jimmy L. Reaves
Director, Southern Research Station,
Forest Service

Acknowledgments

It would be impossible to thank, by name, every individual who contributed to some aspect of this report. However, we would like to acknowledge the invaluable help provided by numerous organizations, individuals in the field, data processors, and scientists without which this report could not have been written.

First and foremost, the authors thank the field crews from both the Tennessee Division of Forestry and the Forest Service, U.S. Department of Agriculture, FIA Program for collecting data across the State. You do not receive enough thanks for the service you provide, without which this report would contain empty pages.

The authors thank the staff of the Division of Forestry, especially Steven Scott and David Arnold, for their participation in the FIA inventory program in Tennessee.

The authors owe thanks to the late Victor Rudis for contributing portions of the "Statistical Reliability" section and "Methods" section in this report.

The authors also thank Roger Conner, Wayne K. Clatterbuck, David Arnold, and Steven Scott for their frank and candid reviews of earlier versions of this report.

The authors owe a great deal of gratitude to Helen Beresford for programming the tools to generate many of the estimates used to populate the tables and figures in this report, and Jeff Turner and Jason Meade for tirelessly helping the entire "Resource Analysis" section make sure we are using the correct data.

Brett Butler, Earl Letherberry, and Mark Brown deserve many thanks for supplying the results from the National Woodland Owner Survey for Tennessee.

The following people were responsible for collecting field data:

Tennessee Division of Forestry

David Arnold
Darren Bailey
Dennis Bradburn
Chris Ellis
John Fenderson
John Ferris
Andy French
Ellen Gray
Jim Gray
Lyn Kuhn
Phil Morrissey
John Muller
John Mullins
Jennifer Myers
Danny Osborne
Stephen Pears
Brian Rucker
Travis Trainor
Scott Vasser

FIA Staff

Brad Bolton
Chad Clark
David Crawford
Lyndell Davidson
Jimmie Dortch
Joseph DiModica
David Fournier
Phillip Fry
Keith Gustafson
Brain Kasper
David Lambert
Chris Mate
Russ Oakes
Matthew Powell
Angie Rowe
Justin Seaborne
Warren Tucker

The following FIA staff were responsible for editing and processing the collected data:

Helen Beresford
Jim Brown
Ali Conner
Linda Heatherly (now retired)
Jason Meade
David Morgan
Ted Ridley
Larry Royer (now retired)
Jeffery Turner

Contents

Contents

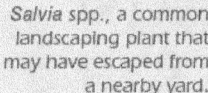

Salvia spp., a common
landscaping plant that
may have escaped from
a nearby yard.

Text Figures

Page

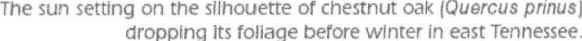

The sun setting on the silhouette of chestnut oak (*Quercus prinus*) dropping its foliage before winter in east Tennessee.

Common fleabane (*Erigeron philadephicus*).

Appendix Figures

Page

Text Tables

Cypress trees grow within the waters of flooded landscapes in west Tennessee.

Positive Developments

• Tennessee's forests covered an estimated 13.78 million acres (52 percent) of the State in 2004.

• Throughout the period from 1961 to 2004, forest land in Tennessee has comprised about one-half of the State's 26 million acres of land.

• Ninety-six percent (13.3 million acres) of Tennessee's forest land was available for timber production in 2004.

• A wide variety of species are found in Tennessee, including hardwoods such as yellow-poplar, oak, hickory, maple, beech, birch, and black locust. Softwood species occurring in the State include shortleaf pine, Virginia pine, loblolly pine, eastern redcedar, cypress, and others. Overall, about 125 separate tree species were recorded between 2000 and 2004.

• Hardwood forest types have dominated the Tennessee landscape in every Forest Inventory and Analysis (FIA) inventory of the State conducted during the period 1948–2004. The estimate of softwood forest acreage produced for the 2004 inventory is the smallest ever published by FIA for Tennessee.

• The oak-hickory forest-type group accounted for 74 percent (10.1 million acres) of the 13.8 million acres of Tennessee forest land in 2004.

• In 2004, red maple was the most common species in terms of number of individual stems recorded on forest land, and the two species with the greatest amount of volume on Tennessee forest land were white oak and yellow-poplar.

• In 2004, about 85 percent of the forest land in Tennessee was in private land holdings. About 9 percent of private land holdings are considered to be within the ownership of forest industry in Tennessee.

Fall foliage in the mountains of east Tennessee.

• Fifteen percent of forest land in Tennessee was publicly administered by local, State, or Federal agencies in 2004. One-third of the public forest land was administered as national forests and one-third by other Federal agencies. The remaining one-third of Tennessee public forest land was owned and administered by various State and local governments.

• In 2004, aesthetics was chosen by landowners (an estimated 252,000 ownerships) as the most important reason they had for owning forest land, followed by family legacy (226,000), nature protection (201,000), and privacy (187,000).

• The overall standing volume of growing stock on timberland in Tennessee increased about 36 percent from 1989 to 2004. That is an average increase in volume of around 2 percent per year. The overall standing inventory is growing larger each year.

• Standing growing-stock volume totaled about 22.6 billion cubic feet in 2004. This represents an increase of about 116 million cubic feet since 1999.

• In 2004, the stands on Tennessee's timberlands were predominantly of natural origin. Consistently from 1989 to 2004, about 96 percent of timberland was of natural origin (i.e., not planted). Planted stands accounted for an estimated 4 percent of timberland area over the same period. In 2004, planted stands accounted for an estimated 497,000 acres across the State.

Interesting Trends

• Early successional or small diameter forest acres (forested stands with primarily small diameter trees) declined over the period 1961–2004.

• Of 18 oak species common in Tennessee, 12 declined in relative stocking levels between 1999 and 2004.

An old field in west Tennessee naturally reverting to a mixed pine hardwood forest.

• The 1999–2002 southern pine beetle (SPB) epidemic was the worst in Tennessee since the 1970s and caused significant financial loses. However, many of the impacted pine forests have either been replanted or have regenerated naturally to predominately hardwood types.

• Between 2000 and 2004, the greatest impact of the SPB was observed in the eastern portion of the State. The highest level of softwood mortality occurred in the east FIA unit.

• FIA estimates that the stand-age distributions for both national forest and other Federal lands are skewed toward the older age classes in Tennessee. In 2004, national forests in Tennessee had the fewest acres of young stands (i.e., those in which the average age of the dominant and codominant stems is 40 years or less) among all ownerships.

• In 2004, young stands accounted for 16 percent of all stands on national forest land, while young stands accounted for 32 percent (3.7 million acres) of forest land in private ownership.

• In 2004, about 96 percent of the State's family-owned forest land was estimated to be in parcels of < 100 acres.

• Although forest land acreage remained relatively unchanged between 1999 and 2004, Tennessee lost productive timberland during the same time period. Timberland declined an estimated 205,000 acres between 1999 and 2004.

• Tree cutting (all forms) occurred on an estimated 1.1 million acres, or 8 percent, of Tennessee timberland between 1999 and 2004.

Issues and Trends to Watch

• The historical trend of increasing forest land acreage in Tennessee appears to have leveled off with the 2004 estimates. Statistically, there was no change in forest land acreage from 1999 to 2004. The leveling off could represent the first sign

of anticipated declines due to fragmentation, parcelization, and associated land-use changes.

• Four oak species (water, swamp chestnut, nuttall, and cherrybark oak), all of which are commonly found in bottomland hardwood communities, have declined in relative stocking by an estimated average annual change near -1 percent per year over the period 1999–2004.

• In 2004, the rarest forest types within the loblolly-shortleaf pine type group were Table Mountain pine and pitch pine, two forest types that are often found in midelevation communities in the Southern Appalachians and Cumberland Plateau. Following the outbreak of the SPB during 1999–2002, these two forest types became increasingly scarce in Tennessee.

• In 2004, the Table Mountain pine type was the rarest softwood forest type defined by FIA in Tennessee, while the hard maple-basswood type was the rarest FIA hardwood forest type.

• Annual softwood net growth decreased from 154 million cubic feet between 1989 and 1998 to 38 million cubic feet during 1999–2004. The decrease in softwood growth appears to have been driven by the SPB outbreak of 1999–2004.

• Fifty-two percent of all forested plots sampled from 2000 to 2004 contained at least one nonnative invasive plant species. Japanese honeysuckle (*Lonicera japonica*) was the most frequently observed species and occurred on 24 percent of all forested subplots (2,322). Nepalese browntop (*Microstegium vimineum*) was the second most common nonnative invasive on sampled subplots.

• The most frequently observed nonnative invasive tree species was tree-of-heaven (*Ailanthus altissima*), which occurred on 6 percent of all forested subplots sampled between 2000 and 2004.

A nonnnative grass, *Microstegium vimineum*, blankets the forest floor impeding the regeneration of native plant species.

Springtime color in Tennessee.

Introduction

This resource bulletin consolidates data from the seventh survey of Tennessee's forest resources which was conducted during the period 2000–2004. Data on the extent, condition, and classification of forest land and associated timber volumes, as well as growth, removals, and mortality rates are described and interpreted. Data on forest health and forest landowner characteristics are also evaluated. Estimates of forest resources are reported at multiple scales. The two most common scales discussed in this report are the State and unit level. The State of Tennessee is divided into five Forest Inventory and Analysis (FIA) units (fig. 1) that approximate broad physiographical sections of the State. The five FIA units are labeled: (1) West, (2) West Central, (3) Central, (4) Plateau, and (5) East.

History of Tennessee's Forest Inventory

Six previous periodic inventories have been completed in Tennessee. The inventories of 1950, 1961, 1971, 1980, 1989, and 1999 provide statistics for measuring changes and trends over the past 55 years. Traditionally, FIA reporting of forest resource statistics has been oriented toward sustaining timber resources to supply the needs of States for forest products. Over time the idea of "sustainability" has evolved from a concept

Native grasses flourishing in a group selection harvest in west Tennessee.

driven by human needs to one that is defined by a diversity of values including timber resources, wildlife habitat, species richness, and cultural benefits, among others. The Forest Service, U.S. Department of Agriculture, FIA Program has evolved alongside the broader concept of sustainability. The FIA Program now reports on a diverse set of variables and attempts to help answer numerous questions surrounding the forest resources of each State in the South, including Tennessee.

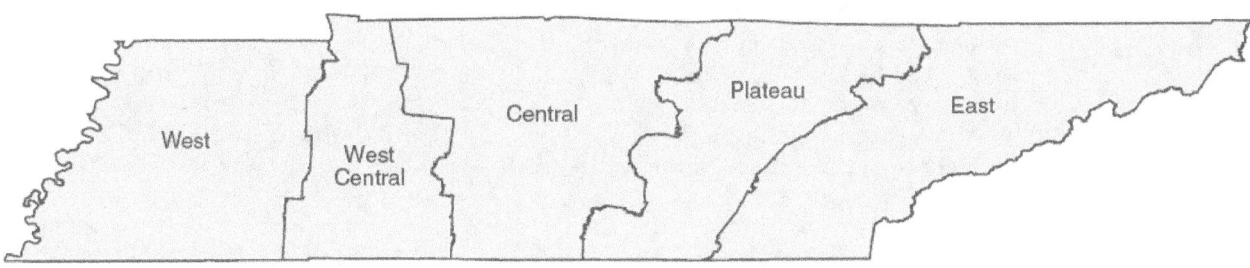

Figure 1—FIA unit boundaries for Tennessee.

Cherokee National Forest.

A New Way to Monitor Forest Resources

In 1999, the FIA of the Southern Research Station and the Tennessee Department of Agriculture, Division of Forestry began implementing the new annual survey strategy in Tennessee. The strategy involves rotating measurements of five systematic samples (or panels), each of which represents about 20 percent of all plots in the State. A panel generally takes 1 year to complete and covers only one growing season. For Tennessee, data collection for all five panels was completed in 5 years. This analysis focuses primarily on changes and trends in recent years and their implications for Tennessee's forests, forest landowners, and citizens. (See the "Data Sources and Techniques" section for further information on data collection methodology).

Updates to the 1999 Estimates

During the last several years, the Forest Service FIA Program has modified some of its procedures in the course of developing a nationally consistent data structure and program. Also, some FIA procedures have changed significantly as technology has advanced. All of this change has the objective of strengthening estimates over time. In some cases, new methods reveal previously unknown bias in historic estimates. That has been the case for the 1999 estimates previously released and published (Schweitzer 2001). For example, FIA has transitioned to the use of an automated stratification procedure that utilizes the National Land Cover Database (NLCD) to aid Phase 1 area stratification in order to reduce the variance in forest land area estimates. The NLCD methods revealed bias in both the 1999 and preliminary 2004 estimates (Coulston 2008) that needed to be corrected. This report includes the updated estimates for 1999 along with the finalized 2004 estimates in order to strengthen the short-term trends.

The State of Tennessee's Forests, 2004

Forces of Change in Tennessee

All living systems, including forests, are characterized by ongoing change. Although forest communities change even when "left alone" or preserved, many forest communities change as a result of forest land disturbance. Disturbances can be natural or human-caused (anthropogenic), can have short-term or long-term impacts, or can be permanent or transitory in nature. Accordingly, the degree of change is a result of the type of disturbance. Disturbances are widespread on the Tennessee landscape and have helped shape the forest land we enjoy today. Furthermore, similar disturbances will help shape the forests we enjoy in the future. Forest land disturbances are a constant force of change in any forested ecosystem. Multiple disturbances, natural and anthropogenic, and autogenic (internal forces, such as competition between trees)

and allogenic (external forces, such as tornadoes), affect forests, often altering their future development or condition. In fact, the post-disturbance forest rarely resembles the community that preceded it. Whether natural or anthropogenic, long-standing or short-term, permanent or transitory, Tennessee's forest lands are constantly experiencing change.

Recently, major sources of change within Tennessee's forests have been human development, nonnative invasive plants, insects, disease, and silvicultural activity. Although some changes in our forests can be viewed as negative, not all change is detrimental to the health of a functioning forest ecosystem; nor do all changes necessarily result in the loss of forest land. For example, while the recent (1999–2002) epidemic outbreak of southern pine beetle (SPB) (*Dendroctonus frontalis*) caused significant financial loses, many of the impacted forests have either been replanted or have regenerated naturally. In either case, a functioning early successional

A forest recovering from the recent (1999–2002) southern pine beetle infestation that significantly impacted softwood forests of Tennessee.

forest is now growing in the place of the older trees. As a result, wildlife species that require early successional habitat can take advantage of this newly established forest land. Similarly, silvicultural activity can provide a young, healthy forest in place of an older or damaged stand. In fact, additional acreage in early successional habitat types can be viewed as a positive development in Tennessee because Tennessee forest land is currently (2004) heavily dominated by mid- to late-successional forests. The State has seen a declining trend in early successional or small diameter forests over the past 40+ years (1961–2004) (fig. 2). In 1971, early successional forests accounted for about 35 percent of all forest land. In 2004, early successional forests accounted for only 12 percent of all forest land.

No one forest type, whether hardwood or softwood, young or old, can satisfy the needs of all forest-dependent organisms. A tapestry of different forest types, structures, ages, and forest conditions is needed to provide the many habitats required by the flora and fauna of Tennessee. Change can give rise to a diversity of habitat types, so change can be positive.

"Not even the wildest forest can serve the habitat needs of all creatures. As forests evolve through time, they provide habitat for different groups of species. As the structure of the forest changes, species move on or die out. That's nature."

Dr. Allan Houston, Forester and Wildlife Biologist, Ames Plantation, Grand Junction, TN, Evergreen, October 1997.

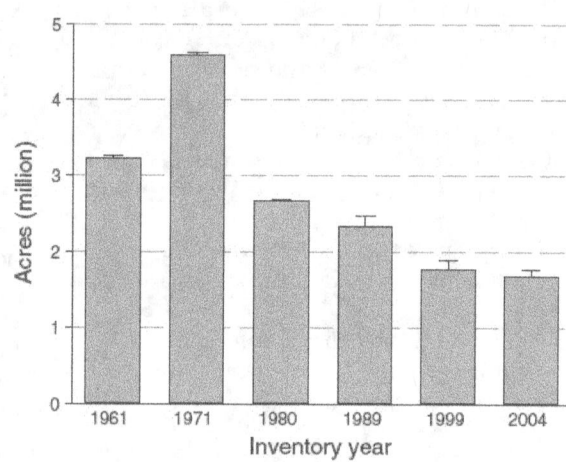

Figure 2—Acreage of sapling-seedling (early successional) forests in Tennessee, 1961–2004. Error bars represent one standard error.

An American green tree frog (*Hyla cinera*) found "hanging out" in a clearcut.

The FIA inventory allows us to begin identifying changes by examining the current condition of the State's forests with respect to trends in land use; stand composition; estimates of forest land acreage and wood volume or biomass; and annual rates of change such as growth, removals, and mortality. In addition, the FIA inventory data can be used in specialized analyses such as analyses of changes in species composition over time. The data show that Tennessee's forests were changing in 2004, but they also show that Tennessee neither gained nor lost total forest land acreage between 1999 and 2004 and that hardwood forests continued to dominate the State's forest area.

Disturbances are a Part of Tennessee Forests

Tennessee forests are heavily influenced by numerous disturbance events. In fact, for the period between 1999 and 2004, an estimated 334,000 acres of timberland in Tennessee were disturbed annually. Thus, at current rates, an area equivalent to the entire forest land area in Tennessee is disturbed about every 41 years. As a result, disturbances are important in defining, shaping, and changing the forests around us within the State. Of course, there are areas within the State, such as deep coves in the Great Smoky Mountains National Park or Dick Cove on the escarpment of the Cumberland Plateau in southeast Tennessee, which can persist without external disturbances for long periods of time. However, maturing forests without external disturbances are influenced by internal changes, particularly as trees age,

senesce, and begin to break-up and fall over. Nevertheless, many areas in Tennessee, such as the table lands of the Middle Cumberland Plateau, can be affected by multiple disturbances over short periods. For example, over a 3-day period in November of 2002, seven different tornadoes touched ground in the Central and/or Plateau units (fig. 3).

Wind related disturbances such as tornados are not the only type of disturbance that impacts Tennessee forests. FIA collects information on over 20 different types of disturbance, including human disturbance other than disturbances through active forest management. During the period 1999–2004 insects, weather, animals, and humans were responsible for the majority of disturbed acreage in Tennessee. The

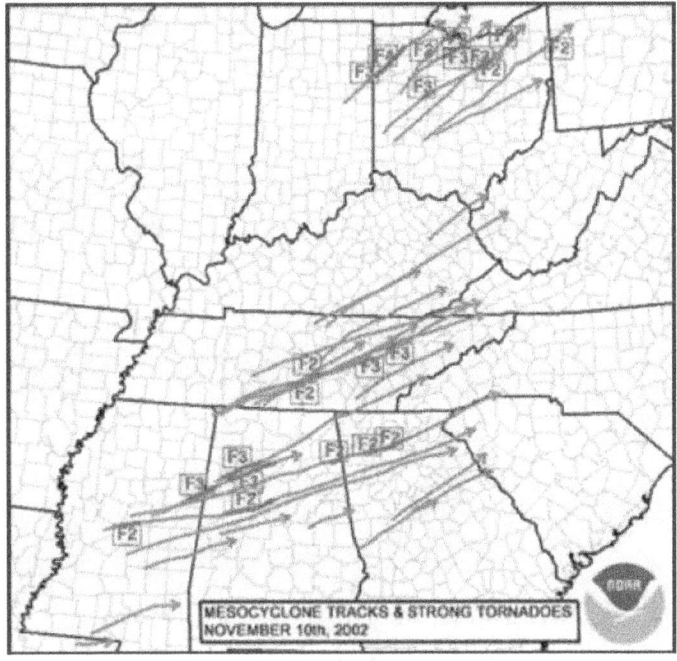

Figure 3—Veterans Day weekend tornado outbreak of 2002 in which 83 tornados touched down in 17 different States. Image of tornado tracks provided by the National Oceanic and Atmospheric Administration. (Source: NOAA 2003)

four categories combined accounted for an estimated 302,000 acres of disturbed timberland annually (fig. 4). Insect disturbances to timberland were estimated to affect 132,000 acres annually, accounting for the largest number of disturbed acres. Weather- and animal- (not including grazing) related disturbances impacted similar acreage, with 65,000 and 62,000 acres disturbed annually, respectively. Disturbances resulting from fire or disease were not as widespread. Fire impacted an estimated 21,000 acres annually, while disease-related disturbances accounted for around 9,000 acres annually (fig. 4).

Insect disturbances were mostly concentrated on the Plateau and in the East (fig. 5). Forty-two percent of the area annually disturbed by insects was located in the Plateau unit, and 55 percent was located in the East unit. The disturbance categories that accounted for the most annually disturbed acres in the West and West Central units were weather and humans. Animal-related disturbances accounted for the majority of the annually disturbed acres in the Central unit, with around 29,000 acres disturbed (fig. 5). Weather-related disturbance was most extensive on the Cumberland Plateau. An estimated 27,000 acres of timberland were disturbed annually in the Plateau unit, which accounted for 42 percent of all weather-related disturbances observed by FIA.

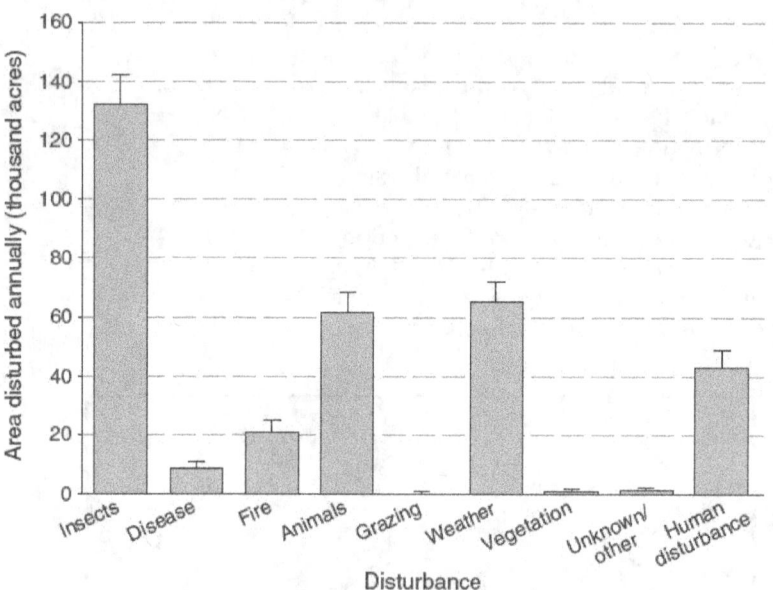

Figure 4—Area of timberland disturbed annually between 1999 and 2004 by disturbance category, Tennessee. Error bars represent one standard error.

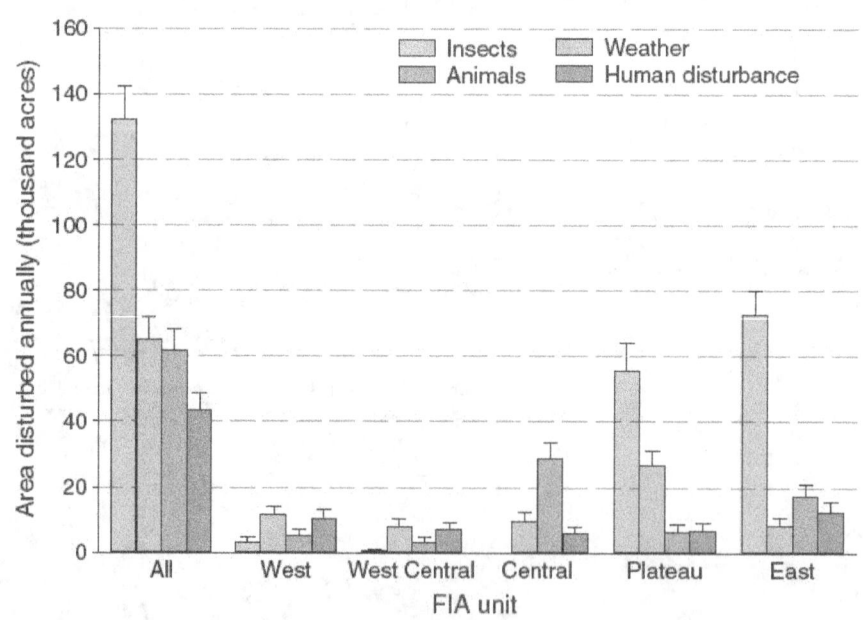

Figure 5—Area of timberland disturbed annually by FIA unit and disturbance category, Tennessee. Error bars represent one standard error.

Special Topic: Southern Pine Beetle in Tennessee

The SPB (fig. 6) is native to Tennessee. Periodically, when environmental conditions are conducive to rapid population increases, SPB populations reach epidemic levels and significant tree mortality can occur (fig. 7). The 1999–2002 epidemic outbreak of SPB was a significant disturbance to the forests of Tennessee. The influence of this event is evident in numerous measures related to the forest resources of Tennessee. For example, you can observe the significant amount of insect-related disturbances in the State between 1999 and 2004 (see figs. 4 and 5). The 1999–2002 epidemic was the worst in Tennessee since the 1970s. The impact is noticeable in numerous estimates throughout this report. While a variety of insects impact Tennessee's forests, the SPB has been appropriately labeled "the most destructive forest insect in the Southern United States" (Cassidy 2005).

Figure 6—Southern pine beetle (*Dendroctonus frontalis*), USA, Mississippi, Winston County, Noxubee N.W. Refuge, 17–24 March 1997, R.A. Tisdale. (Source: Simon Hinkley and Ken Walker, Museum Victoria)

Figure 7—Southern pine beetle infestation in a southern yellow pine forest. (Ronald F. Billings, Texas Forest Service, Bugwood.org)

SPB outbreaks at epidemic levels were recorded in only one Tennessee county in both 1997 and 1998 (fig. 8). In 1999, SPB outbreaks reaching epidemic levels were identified in 17 counties. By the year 2000, 48 counties reported infestations at epidemic levels. The number of counties reporting epidemic level infestations peaked at 55 in 2001, decreased to 45 in 2002, and fell to 13 in 2003. By the year 2004, the epidemic infestation was over with only one county reporting an outbreak at epidemic levels.

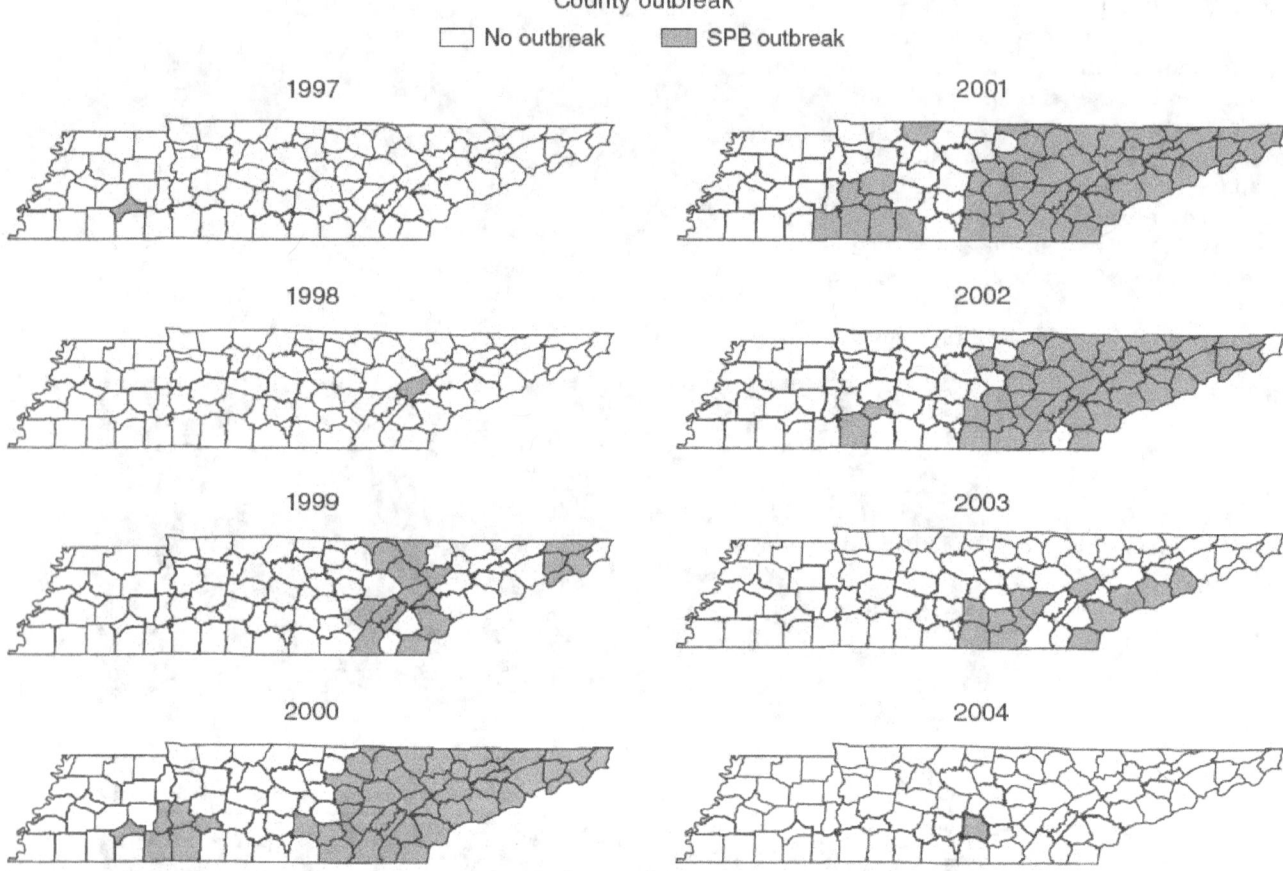

Figure 8—Counties with epidemic level outbreaks of southern pine beetle in Tennessee from 1997 to 2004. (Source: Pye, John M.; Price, Terry S.; Clarke, Stephen R.; Huggett, Robert J., Jr. A history of southern pine beetle outbreaks in the Southeastern United States though 2004. [www.srs.fs.usda.gov/econ/data]).

The SPB epidemic of 1999–2002 affected about 350,000 acres of pine timber with a value of over $350 million (Cassidy 2005). The greatest impact was observed in the East unit where an average of 8.5 million trees per year were lost to some type of mortality (fig. 9). The Plateau unit lost an average of 6.3 million trees per year. Additionally, softwood mortality appears to have been concentrated in the northern section of the Plateau unit and the southern section of the East unit (fig. 10). Not all of the softwood mortality is attributed to the SPB, but the majority of disturbed stands in Tennessee were impacted by insects (fig. 5). Therefore, it is reasonable to infer that the majority of the observed softwood mortality is linked to insect activity and the SPB.

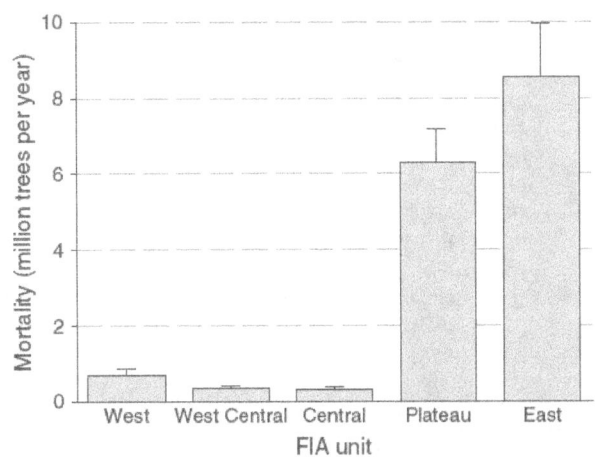

Figure 9—Softwood mortality (number of trees per year) across each FIA unit in Tennessee, 1999–2004. Error bars represent one standard error.

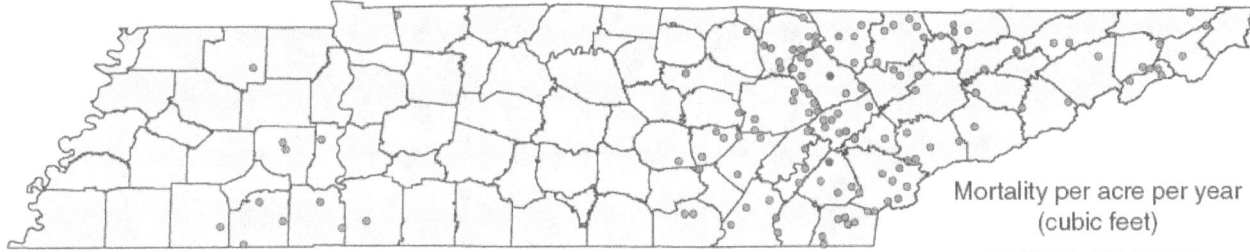

Figure 10—Rate of softwood mortality in Tennessee, 1999–2004.

Mortality per acre per year (cubic feet)

- 45.00001–159.00000
- 159.00001–343.00000
- 343.00001–835.00000
- 835.00001–1,751.00000

A regenerating stand of natural pine below older pine trees that succumbed to the southern pine beetle (*Dendroctonus frontalis*), a natural insect that can sometimes cause significant mortality among many pines species common in Tennessee.

Diversity of Tennessee's Forests

Forests play a vital role in Tennessee's economic, cultural, and biological landscape. The dependence of Tennesseans on the State's forests requires that attention be paid to the extent and condition of the forests. Although the term biological diversity (biodiversity) refers to all aspects of the forest ecosystem, from trees to insects to genetics, this report focuses solely on trees as they relate to forest biodiversity.

Extent and Distribution of Forests

Tennessee's forests covered an estimated 13.78 million acres (52 percent) of the State in 2004 (table 1). In 1999, forests covered an estimated 13.85 million acres, about 247,000 acres more than they covered in 1989. Although it appears that forest land area decreased by about 66,000 acres between 1999 and 2004, the 2004 estimate statistically represents no change and is better viewed as a "leveling off" of the historical trend of increasing forest land since 1971 (fig. 11). The

Table 1—Area for each land class for Tennessee from 1961 to 2004

| Land class | Year | | | | | |
	1961	1971	1980	1989	1999	2004
	thousand acres					
Timberland	13,432.4	12,819.8	12,879.0	13,265.2	13,459.2	13,254.0
Other/reserved	263.5	316.5	429.5	337.3	390.3	530.1
Total forest	13,695.9	13,136.3	13,308.5	13,602.5	13,849.5	13,784.0
Nonforest land	12,826.2	13,338.6	13,141.6	12,844.5	12,511.4	12,504.2
Total land area	26,522.1	26,474.9	26,450.1	26,447.0	26,360.9	26,378.8
	percent					
Forested	52	50	50	51	53	52

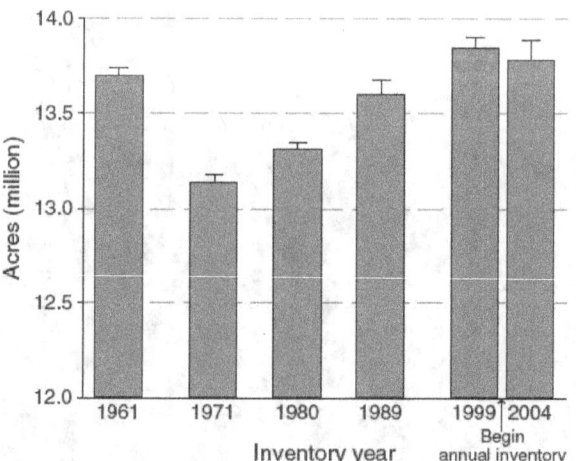

Figure 11—Estimates of forest land in Tennessee with associated standard errors, 1961–2004. Error bars represent one standard error. Note: Y-axis does not begin at zero.

leveling off could represent the first sign of anticipated declines due to fragmentation, parcelization, and associated land use changes. Forest land made up about one-half of the State's 26 million acres of land area throughout the period 1961–2004. During that period, the fraction of land area that was forested increased slightly, from an estimated low of 50 percent in the 1970s to an estimated 53 percent in the 1999 inventory. Concomitantly, the number of FIA plots defined as forested increased between 1989 and 2004 (fig. 12). In 2004, 96 percent (13.3 million acres) of the State's forest land was considered available for timber production.

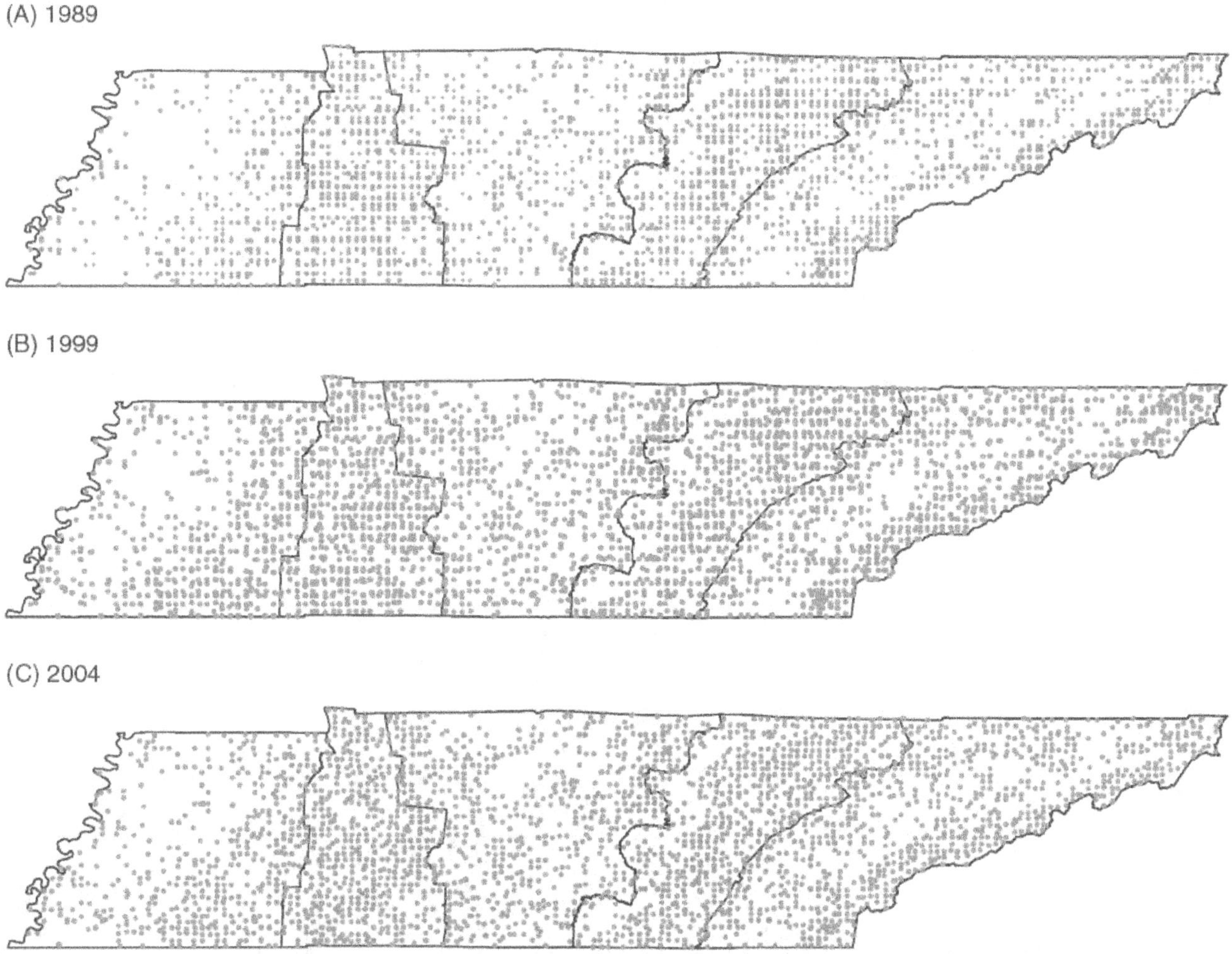

(A) 1989

(B) 1999

(C) 2004

Figure 12—Forested plots in Tennessee, (A) 1989, (B) 1999, and (C) 2004. Plot locations are not true locations. Dots represent the latitude and longitude of FIA "fuzzed and swapped" plots. To safeguard landowner privacy, FIA does not print maps with the actual plot locations represented.

Stand Age

Tennessee's forest stands vary widely in age. In 1999, the 5-year age class that contained the greatest acreage was the 46–50 year age class (fig. 13). By 2004, the peak in the age class distribution had shifted to the 56–60 year age class. Acreage in most younger age classes declined between 1999 and 2004, while acreage in many of the older age classes increased. These results suggest that the Tennessee forest resource was ageing in 2004. More and more stands have recruited into older age classes during the period 1999–2004 which has resulted in a mature forest with fewer and fewer acres in age classes that would be considered early successional.

Tennessee: A Hardwood State

The species composition of a forested stand defines its character, likely future development, ecosystem function, and dynamics as well as providing insight into its historical evolution. For this reason, analyses of current and past species composition aid in understanding the existing forest character and potential developmental pathways.

A wide variety of species are found in Tennessee including hardwoods such as yellow-poplar, oak, hickory, maple, beech, birch, and black locust. Softwood species occurring in the State include shortleaf pine, Virginia pine, loblolly pine, eastern redcedar, cypress, and others. Overall, about 125 separate tree species were recorded during the 2004 forest inventory. Red maple was the most common species in terms of number of individual stems recorded on forest land (fig. 14), and the two species with the greatest amount of volume on Tennessee forest land were white oak and yellow-poplar (fig. 15). It is important to note, however, that all

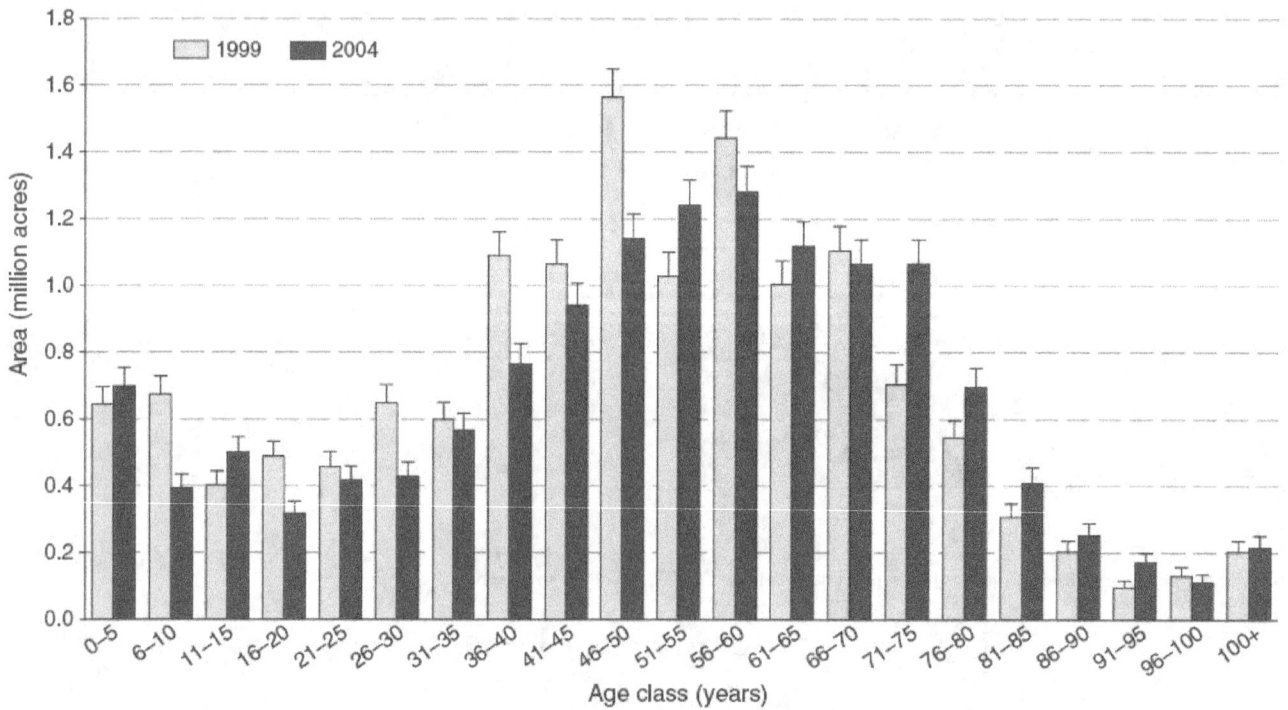

Figure 13—Area of forest land by 5-year age class for Tennessee, 1999 and 2004. Error bars represent one standard error.

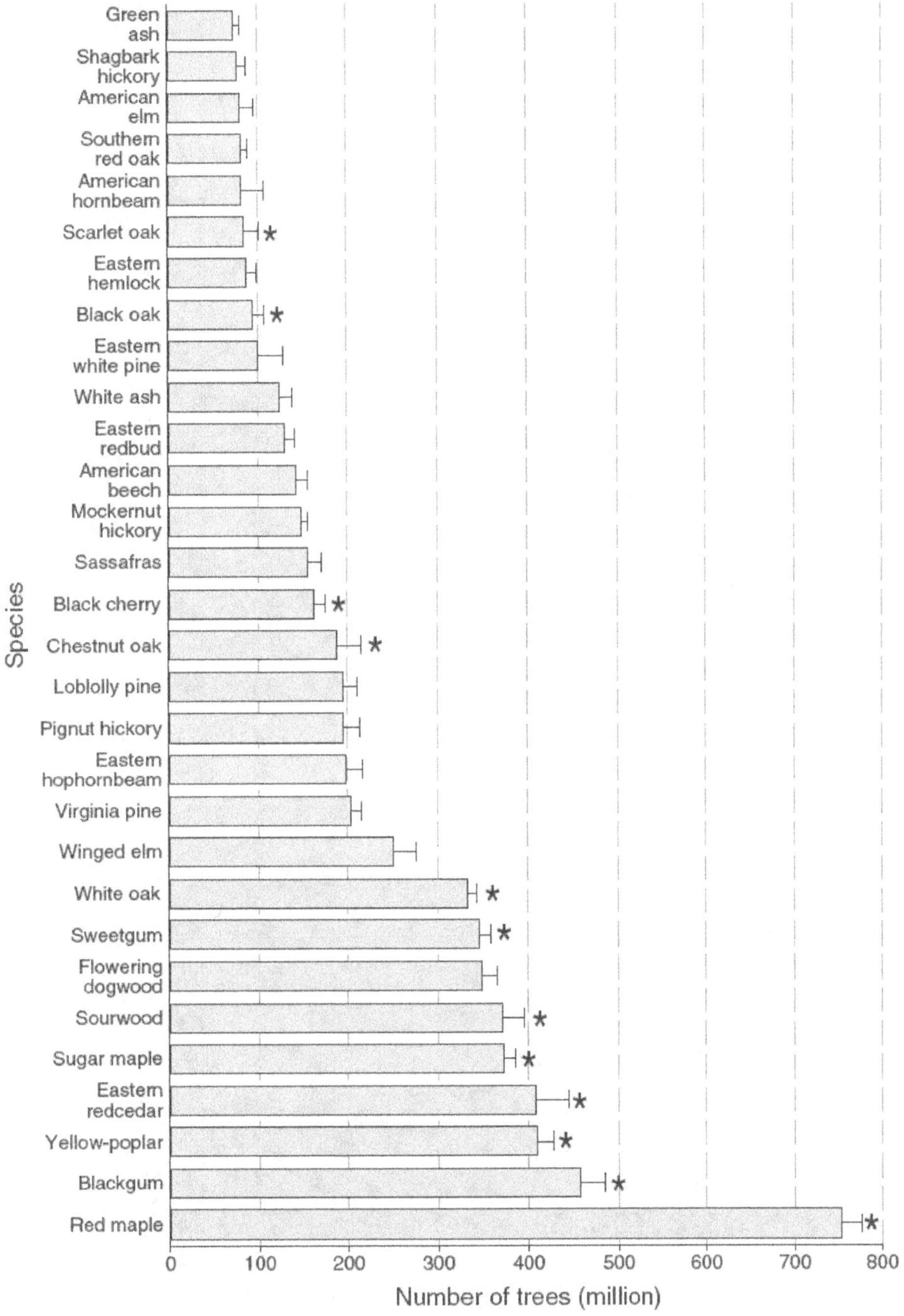

Figure 14—Estimated number of all live trees for common tree species in Tennessee, 2004. Error bars represent one standard error. ★ = High frequency tree species— those species found on the greatest number of forested plots in the State.

13

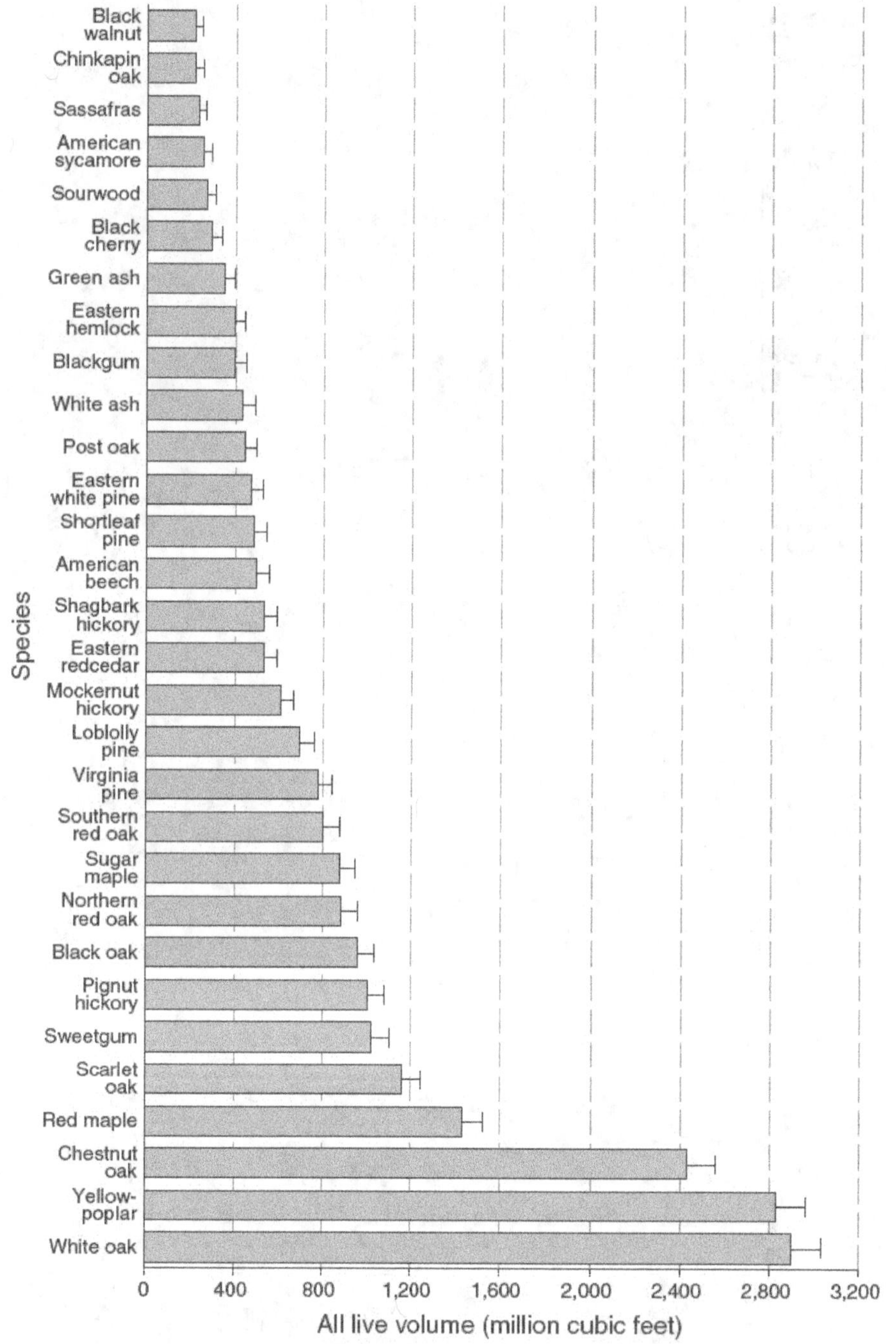

Figure 15—Estimated volume (total cubic feet) for all live trees of common tree species in Tennessee, 2004. Error bars represent one standard error.

oak species combined comprise a very substantial proportion of the total estimated volume. White oak, red maple and yellow-poplar were also three of the most widely distributed species in the State (fig. 16). Figure 16 also shows the geographical distribution of some other interesting and/or important tree species in Tennessee.

No one tree species dominates Tennessee's forest land in terms of both numbers of live trees and volume. The statistics more or less reflect the ecological niches and silvical characteristics of the common species found in the State. Species such as yellow-poplar, white oaks, and many in the red oak group comprise the larger canopy species in much of the forest. Some of the more numerous species, such as red maple, flowering dogwood, and eastern redbud are smaller, but generally occupy the midstory and understory in greater numbers.

Hardwood forest types have dominated the Tennessee landscape in every inventory of the State produced by FIA (fig. 17).

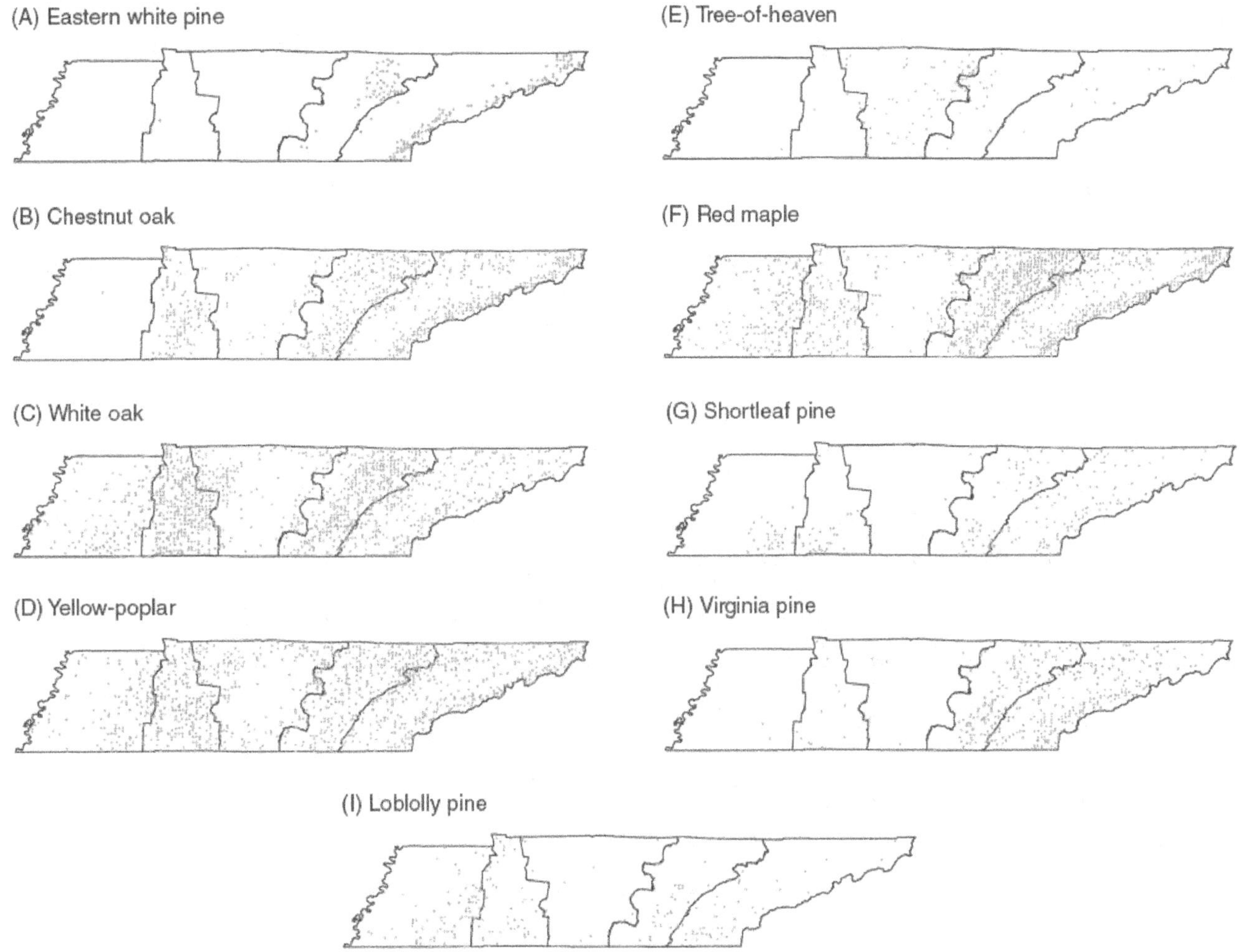

(A) Eastern white pine

(E) Tree-of-heaven

(B) Chestnut oak

(F) Red maple

(C) White oak

(G) Shortleaf pine

(D) Yellow-poplar

(H) Virginia pine

(I) Loblolly pine

Figure 16—Species distribution maps for important and/or interesting species found in Tennessee, 2004, (A) eastern white pine, (B) chestnut oak, (C) white oak, (D) yellow-poplar, (E) tree-of-heaven, (F) red maple, (G) shortleaf pine, (H) Virginia pine, and (I) loblolly pine. Dots represent the latitude and longitude of FIA "fuzzed and swapped" plots. To safeguard landowner privacy, FIA does not print maps with the actual plot locations represented.

Softwood forest acreage was lower at the time of the 2004 inventory than it was at the time of any other FIA inventory of Tennessee forests. Softwood forest types have been mostly limited to mid- and high-elevational communities of the Appalachian Mountains, the Southern Cumberland Plateau in the east, and the Gulf Coastal Plain in the southwestern part of the State (fig. 18).

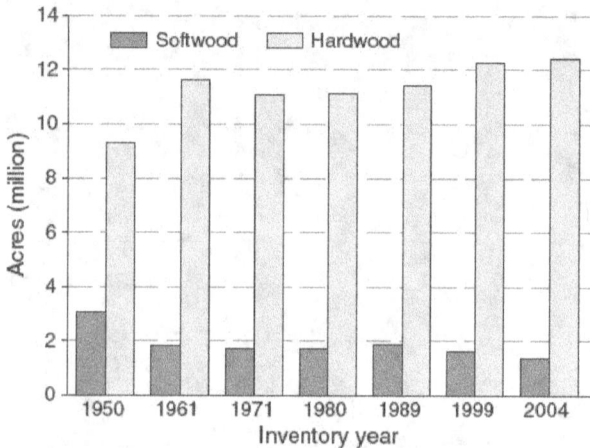

Figure 17—Major forest-type groups for Tennessee, 1950–2004.

Composition of Tennessee Forests

In 2004, the oak-hickory forest-type group accounted for 74 percent (10.1 million acres) of the 13.8 million acres of Tennessee forest land (fig. 19). The oak-hickory forest-type group was also the most widely distributed forest-type group in the State (fig. 20). The oak-pine, loblolly-shortleaf pine, elm-ash-cottonwood, and eastern redcedar forest-type groups accounted for 1.1 million, 875,000, 623,000, and 357,000 acres, respectively. The eastern redcedar forest-type group, while found across the State, was mainly concentrated in central Tennessee within the Inner and Outer Nashville Basins (fig. 21). Cedar glades and other cedar-dominated communities are common in the Nashville Basin ecoregions (fig. 22) (Baskin and Baskin 2003). In 2004, the least extensive forest-type groups within the State were exotic hardwoods (nonnative species such as paulownia and mimosa) and spruce-fir with an estimated 4,000 and 12,000 acres across the State, respectively.

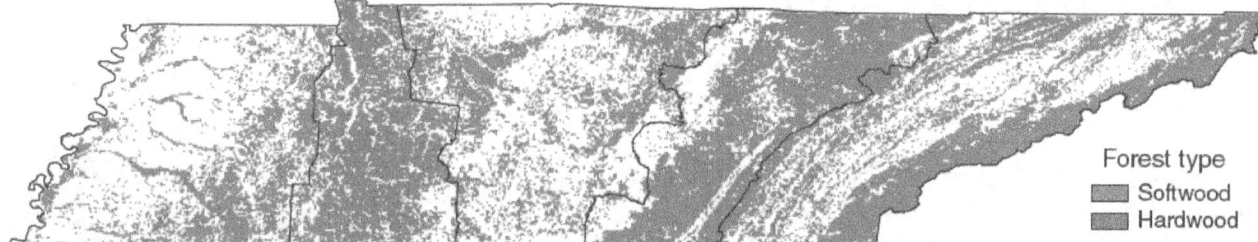

Figure 18—Distribution of hardwood and softwood forest types in Tennessee. Adapted from the 2001 National Land Cover Data (Homer and others 2007).

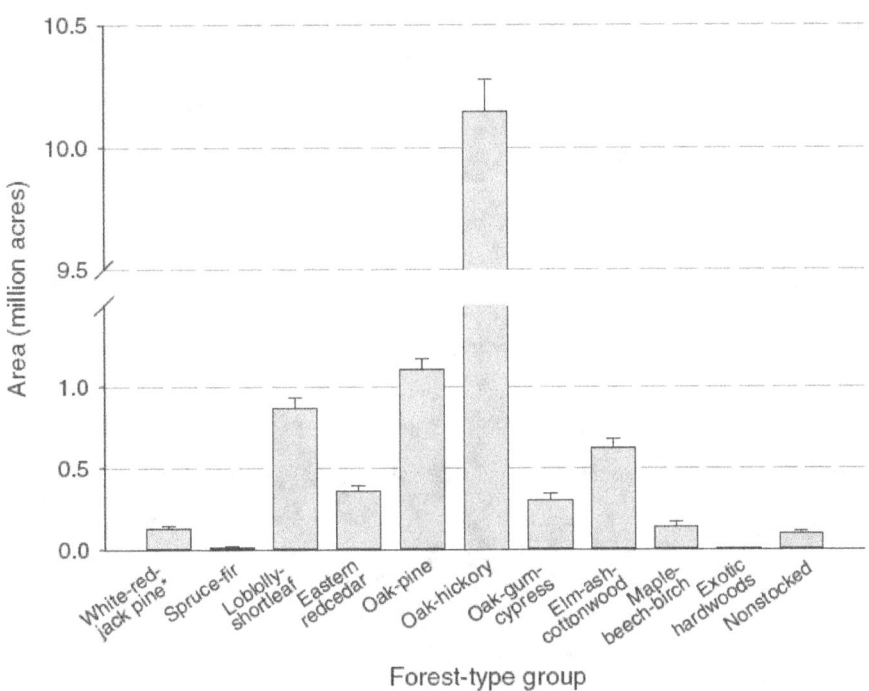

Figure 19—Area of forest land in Tennessee by forest-type group, 2004. Error bars represent one standard error. Note: the break in the Y-axis. * Comprised of eastern white pine and hemlock spp. in Tennessee.

Oak-hickory forest-type group

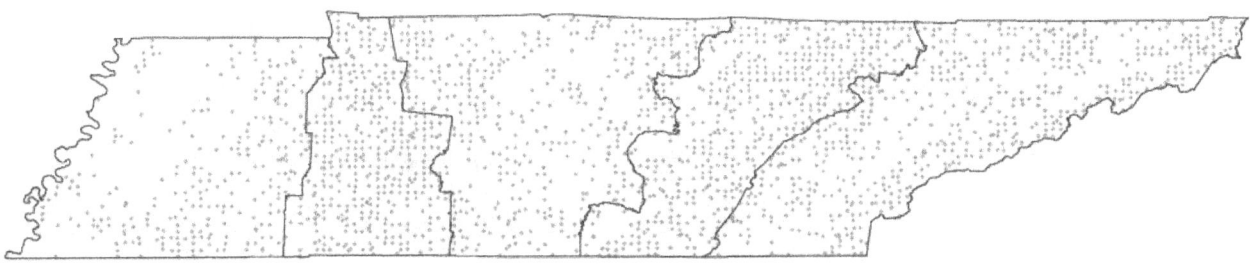

Figure 20—Distribution of plots classified as the oak-hickory forest-type group in Tennessee, 2004. Dots represent the latitude and longitude of FIA "fuzzed and swapped" plots. To safeguard landowner privacy, FIA does not print maps with the actual plot locations represented.

Eastern redcedar forest-type group

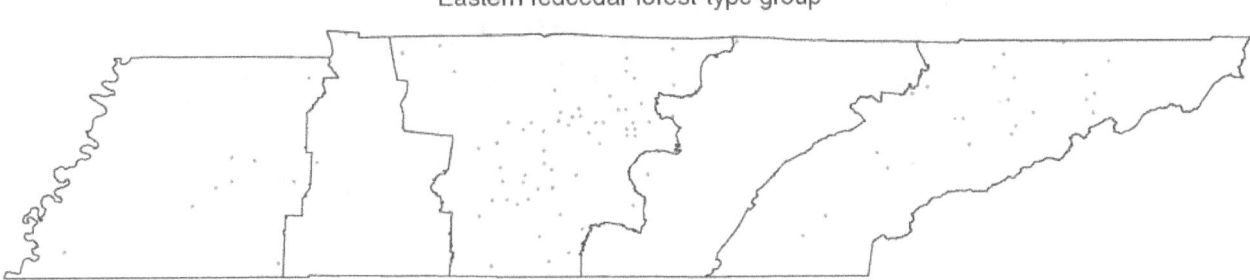

Figure 21—Distribution of plots classified as the eastern redcedar (pinyon-juniper) forest-type group in Tennessee, 2004. Dots represent the latitude and longitude of FIA "fuzzed and swapped" plots. To safeguard landowner privacy, FIA does not print maps with the actual plot locations represented.

However, acreage estimates for forest-type groups with such rarity are accompanied by significant error rates (fig. 19).

The loblolly-shortleaf forest-type group consists of five forest types in Tennessee: (1) loblolly pine, (2) Virginia pine, (3) shortleaf pine (4) pitch pine, and (5) Table Mountain pine. In 2004, the loblolly pine type (452,000 acres) accounted for the majority of area occupied by the loblolly-shortleaf pine type group, followed by Virginia pine, which occupied an estimated 314,000 acres (fig. 23). In 2004, the scarcest forest types within the loblolly-shortleaf pine type group are Table Mountain pine and pitch pine, two forest types that are often found in midelevation communities in the Southern Appalachians and Cumberland Plateau.

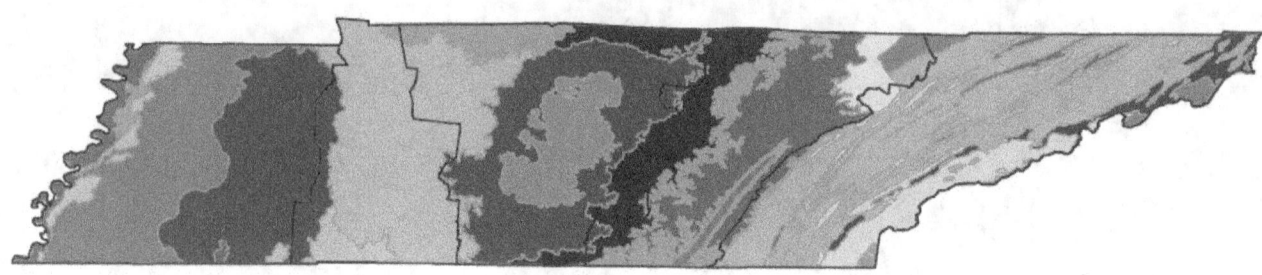

EPA Level IV Ecoregions

Amphibolite mountains	Northern Pleistocene valley trains
Blackland prairie	Outer Nashville Basin
Bluff hills	Plateau escarpment
Broad basins	Sequatchie Valley
Cumberland Mountain thrust block	Southern crystaline ridges and mountains
Cumberland Plateau	Southern dissected ridges and knobs
Dissected Appalachian Plateau	Southern limestone/dolomite valleys and low rolling hills
Eastern Highland Rim	Southern metasedimentary mountains
Fall line hills	Southern sandstone ridges
Flatwoods/Blackland Prairie margins	Southern sedimentary ridges
High mountains	Southern shale valleys
Inner Nashville Basin	Southern table plateaus
Limestone valleys and coves	Transition hills
Loess plains	Western Highland Rim
Northern hilly Gulf Coastal Plain	Western Pennyroyal karst plain
Northern Holocene meander belts	

Ecoregion overlay: Principal Authors: Glenn Griffith (USEPA), James Omernik (USEPA), and Sandra Azevedo (OAO Corporation).

Collaborators and contributors: John Jenkins (NRCS), Richard Livingston (NRCS), James Keys (USFS); Phil Stewart (TDEC), Greg Russell (TDEC), Alan Woods (Dynamac Corporation), Joy Broach (TDEC), Linda Cartwright (TDEC), Debbie Arnwine (Tennessee Department of Health), and Thomas Loveland (USGS).

Figure 22—Ecoregions of Tennessee. (Source: Environmental Protection Agency Level IV Ecoregions of the United States.)

Following the outbreak of the SPB, these two forest types appear to be scarcer on the Tennessee landscape than before.

The oak-hickory forest-type group covers the largest overall area in the State. This group consists of 15 different forest types in Tennessee. In 2004, the six most common forest types within the oak-hickory type group were: (1) white oak-red oak-hickory, (2) mixed upland hardwoods, (3) chestnut oak-black oak-scarlet oak, (4) yellow-poplar-white oak-red oak, (5) chestnut oak, and (6) sweetgum-yellow-poplar. The white oak-red oak-hickory forest type was the most extensive, occupying an estimated 3.7 million acres in the State (fig. 24). Some of the hardwood forest types with the most limited coverage were northern red oak, black walnut, black locust and cottonwood; it is estimated that these types accounted for 48,000, 26,000, 17,000 and 7,000 acres, respectively.

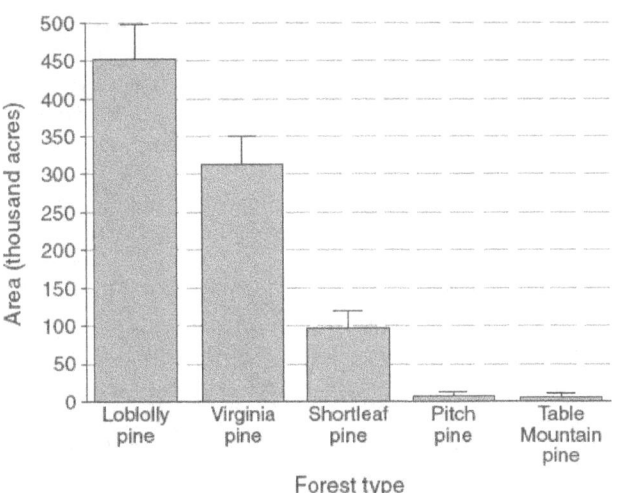

Figure 23—Area of forest land for each forest type within the loblolly-shortleaf pine forest-type group, Tennessee, 2004. Error bars represent one standard error.

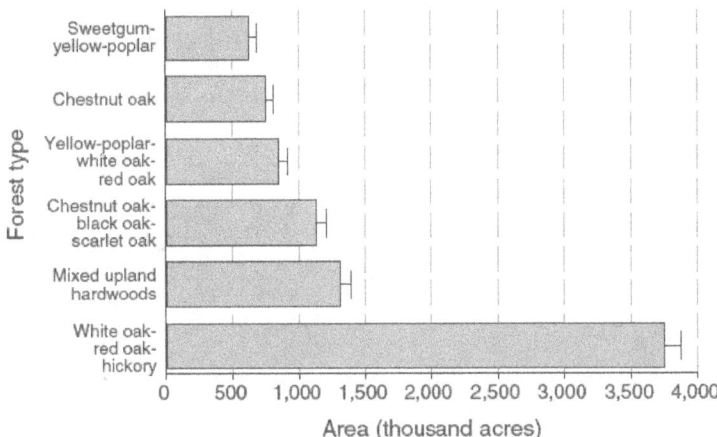

Figure 24—Area of forest land for the six most common forest types within the oak-hickory forest-type group, Tennessee 2004. Error bars represent one standard error.

The new leaves of the year on a southern red oak (*Quercus falcata* var. *falcata*).

Hardwood Forests are Changing

As of 2004, Tennessee remains a State dominated by hardwood forests. However, these forests are changing. Shifts in the species composition of the State's forests are occurring. An analysis of the change in a species' relative stocking over time can indicate the extent to which a species is either gaining or losing ground in a particular system. Information about such changes can help scientists and managers understand the current status of a forested system and predict future compositional shifts. Changes in relative stocking values of common tree species in Tennessee from 1999 to 2004 were investigated by tracking the annualized change (or average annual change).

Average annual change (AAC) for the period between 1999 and 2004 was calculated for each remeasured plot by subtracting the relative stocking (in percent) of each species in 2004 from the relative stocking in 1999 for the same species and dividing that difference by the time period between the plot samples. Figure 25 shows the AAC for some of the most common tree species in Tennessee. The largest positive changes, or increases in plot-level relative stocking, were those calculated for black cherry, yellow-poplar, sugar maple, and red maple (0.32, 0.19, 0.14, and 0.11 percent annually, respectively) (fig. 25). The largest negative values of AAC in relative stocking were those calculated for black oak, northern red oak, and chestnut oak (-0.30, -0.29, and -0.08, respectively). Moreover, of 18 oak species common to Tennessee, 12 had an estimated AAC that was negative. Four oak species, all of which are commonly found in bottomland hardwood communities (water, swamp chestnut, nuttall, and cherrybark), have an estimated AAC near or > -1 percent per year (fig. 26), which indicates a potential for loss of oaks in many bottomland hardwood forest systems.

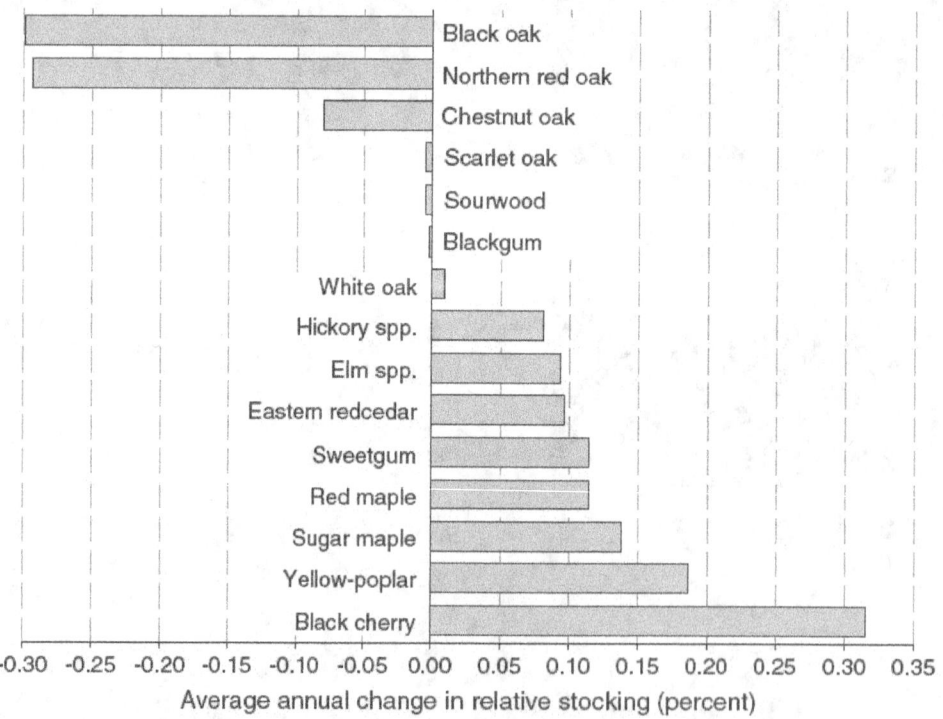

Figure 25—Average annual change in relative stocking (percent) for 15 common tree species in Tennessee for the period between 1999 and 2004.

Tennessee's softwood forests are changing also. All of the six pine species (*Pinus* spp.) sampled in Tennessee in 1999 and 2004 lost ground ecologically during that period (fig. 27).

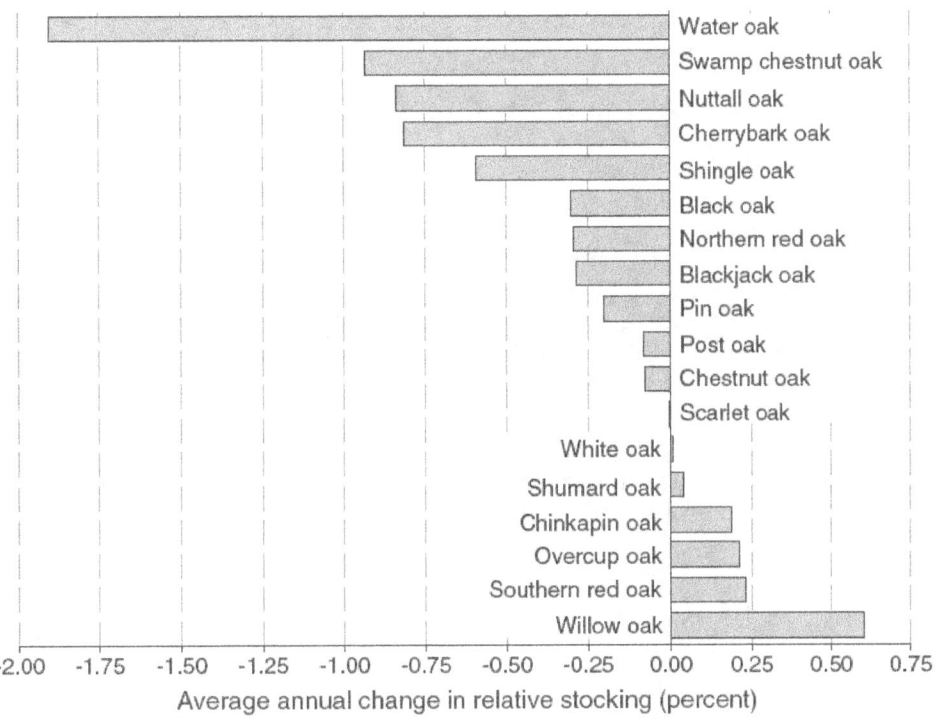

Figure 26—Average annual change in relative stocking (percent) for oak (*Quercus*) species common in Tennessee for the period between 1999 and 2004.

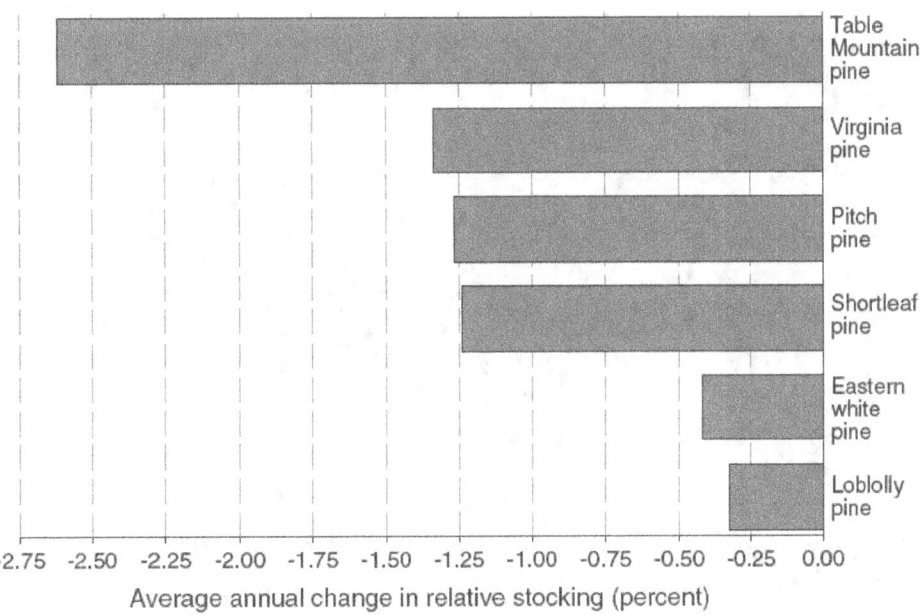

Figure 27—Average annual change in relative stocking (percent) for six pine (*Pinus*) species in Tennessee between 1999 and 2004.

Forest Ownership Patterns in Tennessee

The Forest Service FIA Program collects information about ownership of forested land in each Southern State. Ownership at each forested Phase 2 (see "Glossary") ground plot is determined from publicly available records at local county courthouses. Area, density, and volume estimates are displayed by ownership classes such as nonindustrial private forest land (NIPF), public (including the Forest Service), and forest industry (defined as forest landowners who also own a wood processing facility). Additionally, a National Woodland Owner Survey (NWOS) is sent to each owner, and this survey asks each owner to provide detailed information about his or her objectives for owning forest land (Butler and others 2005).

According to the 2004 inventory, private individuals own 85 percent (11.75 million acres) of the forest land in Tennessee (fig. 28). Concomitantly, 15 percent of the forest land in Tennessee is publicly administered by local, State, or Federal agencies. One-third of the public forest land is administered as national forests and one-third by other Federal agencies. The remaining 5 percent of Tennessee forest land is owned and administered by various State and local governments. The majority of the forest land owned and administered by the Forest Service is within the Cherokee National Forest in the East unit (fig. 29).

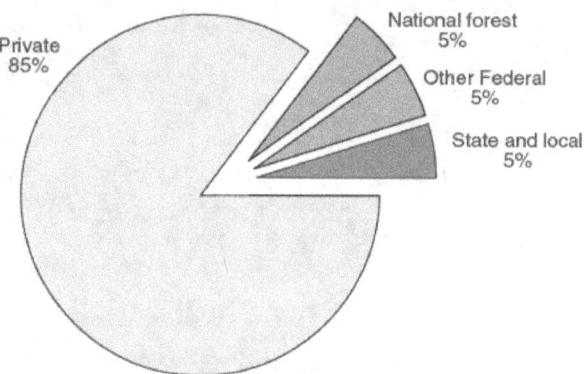

Total forest land = 13.8 million acres

Figure 28—Percent of forest land area by ownership in Tennessee, 2004.

Recreation is a common reason for many Tennessee forest landowners to own forest land.

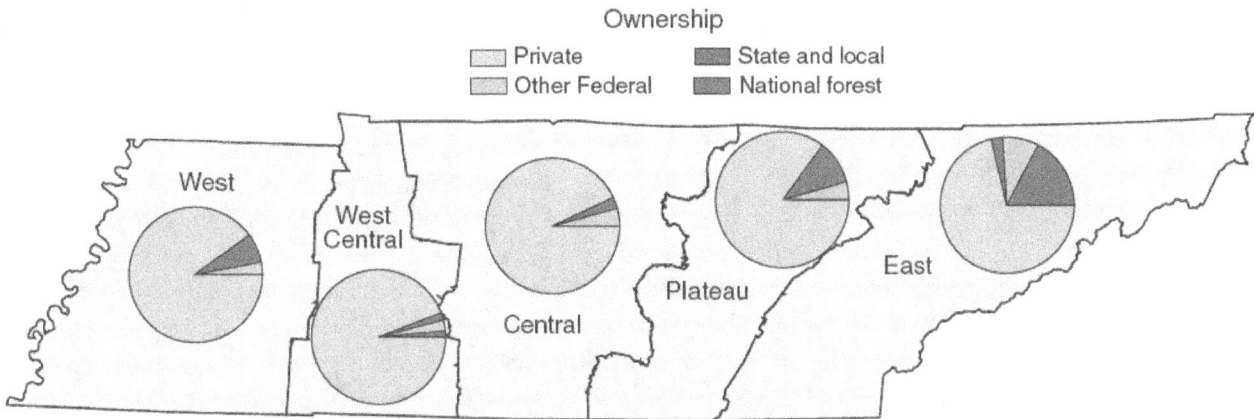

Figure 29—Percent of forest land area by ownership for each FIA unit in Tennessee, 2004.

In 2004, about 665,000 acres of Tennessee forest land was owned and managed by the national forests. Only six forest-type groups were inventoried on national forest land: (1) white-red-jack pine, (2) loblolly-shortleaf pine, (3) eastern redcedar, (4) oak-pine, (5) oak-hickory, and (6) maple-beech-birch (fig. 30). The majority of the national forest land is within the oak-hickory forest-type group. NIPF forest land is extremely diverse, representing nine different forest-type groups. The spruce-fir forest-type group is only found in the other Federal land category. Currently, the largest population of the spruce-fir type group is found in the Great Smoky Mountains National Park in East Tennessee. Similarly, the maple-beech-birch forest-type group is primarily found on Federal lands (fig. 30).

According to the 2004 inventory, the largest acreage of forest land across the State of Tennessee falls in the 56–60 year age class (see discussion on "Stand Age"). However, the distribution of forest land acreage across stand-age classes is not similar among forest land ownership categories (fig. 31). According to FIA estimates, the stand-age distributions for both national forests and other Federal lands are skewed toward the

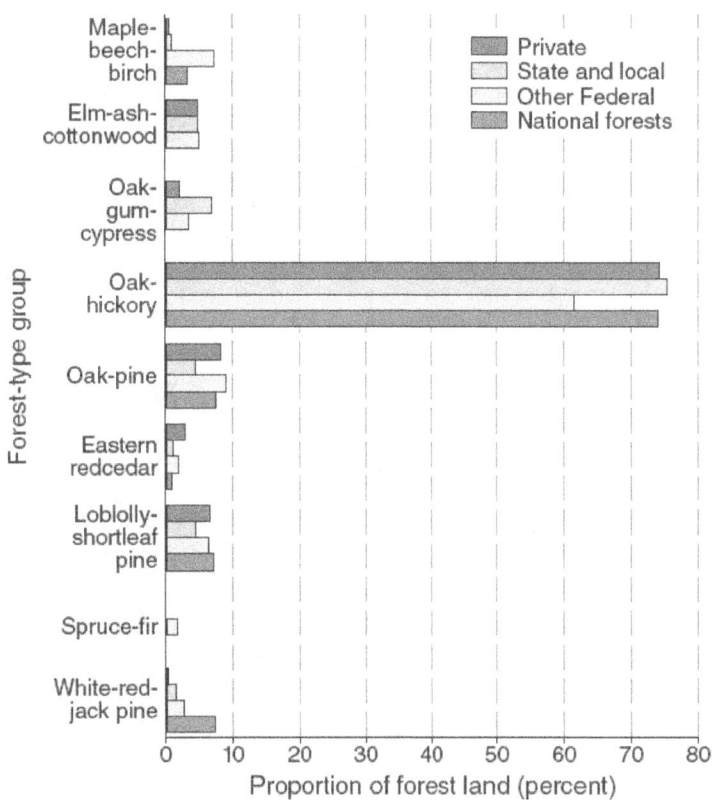

Figure 30—Proportion of forest land in each forest-type group across Tennessee by ownership group, 2004.

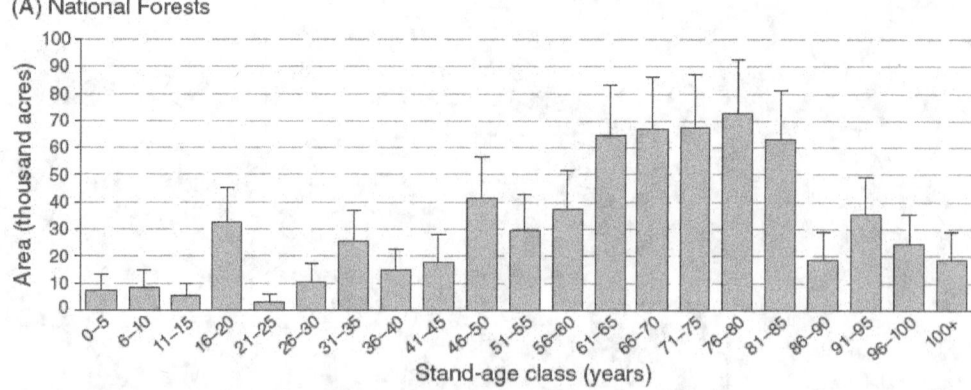

(A) National Forests

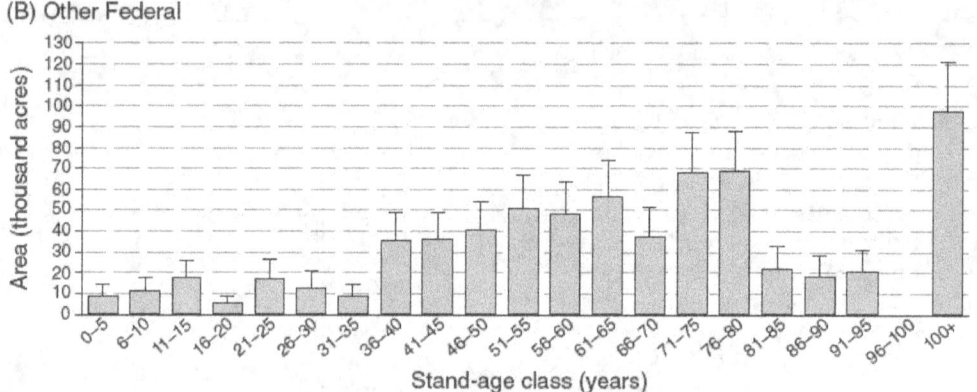

(B) Other Federal

Figure 31—Area of forest land by 5-year stand-age class, Tennessee, 2004, (A) National forests, (B) other Federal lands, (C) State and local lands, and (D) private forest land. Error bars represent one standard error.

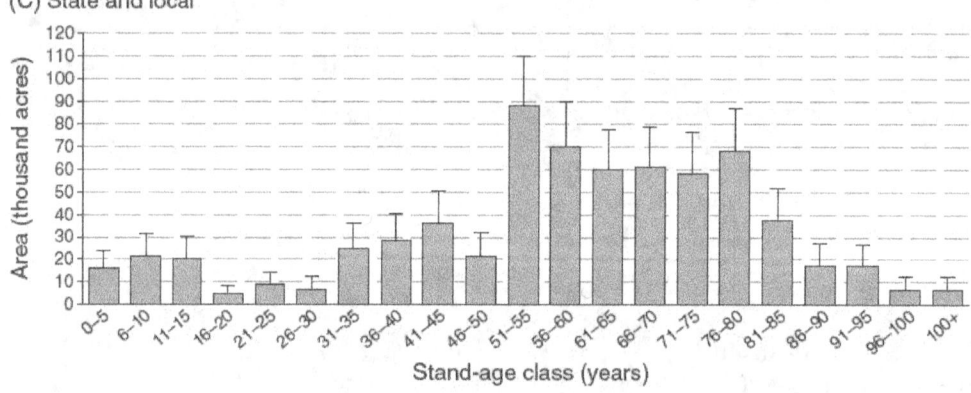

(C) State and local

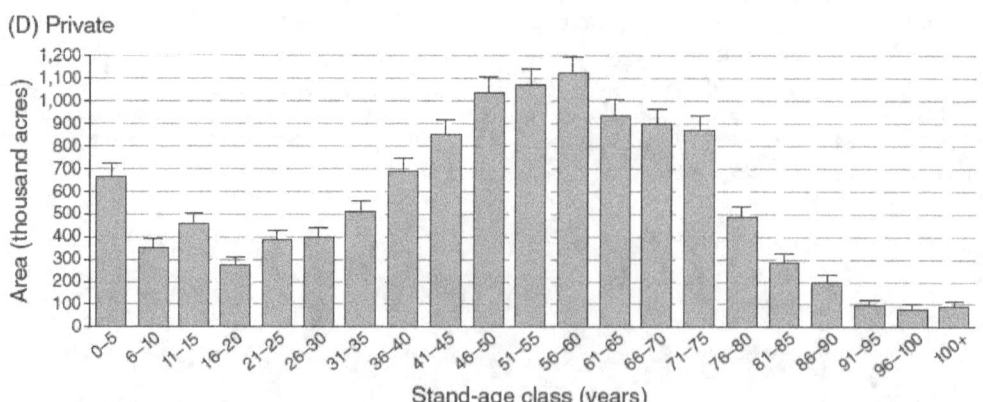

(D) Private

older age classes. In fact, national forests in Tennessee have the fewest acres of young stands (defined 40 years of age or less of the dominant and codominant stems) among all ownerships. Young stands account for 16 percent of all stands on national forest land (fig. 31), while young stands account for 32 percent (3.7 million acres) of forest land in private ownerships. On the other hand, the oldest stands (> 100 years in age) are primarily on other Federal lands (fig. 31B) and private forest land, accounting for 98,000 and 93,000 acres, respectively.

Results from the National Woodland Owner Survey

According to the NWOS conducted in Tennessee between 2002 and 2004 (labeled with the date of 2004), the majority of Tennessee's forest land is in private hands. Results from the 2004 NWOS show that there are an estimated 459,000 private forest landowners in Tennessee (table 2). The likelihood that a given tract of private forest land is managed depends on a wide array of factors, including the number of acres owned and the reasons for owning the land. The 2004 results indicate that most private forest landowners in Tennessee have relatively small holdings. In fact, 96 percent of the State's family-owned forest land was estimated to be in parcels of < 100 acres (table 2). In general, harvesting costs per unit area increase as the size of landholdings decline. Large landholdings (> 5,000 acres) can reasonably be assumed to be available for timber harvesting, but < 1,000 of Tennessee's 459,000 private forest land ownerships were in this category in 2004. Opportunities for harvesting diminish with decreasing parcel size, and forested parcels below a given size threshold typically are not considered viable for commercial forestry activities. For this reason, the 271,000 family-owned forest ownerships estimated to be in parcels < 10 acres in 2004 were probably unavailable for sustained timber production.

In 2004, the great majority of Tennessee family forest ownerships had tenure of ≥ 10 years (table 3). While about 12 percent of survey respondents (an estimated 55,000 ownerships) did not indicate how long their forest had been in their ownership, 85 percent of survey respondents (an estimated 404,000 ownerships) did answer. Of those that supplied tenure information, 30 percent indicated they had owned their land between 10 and 24 years. Only 2 percent of family forest ownerships had tenure > 50 years (table 3).

Table 2—Estimated number of family-owned forests in Tennessee by size of forest landholdings, 2004

Size of forest landholdings	Ownerships			Sample size
	Number	Standard error	Percent	
acres	- - - - thousand - - - -			count
1–9	271	90	59.0	15
10–49	139	20	30.4	49
50–99	29	5	6.4	34
100–499	18	2	3.9	50
500–999	1	<1	0.2	12
1,000–4,999	<1	<1	<0.1	12
5,000+	<1	<1	<0.1	6
Total	459	88	100.0	178

Numbers in columns may not sum to totals due to rounding.

Table 3—Estimated number of family-owned forests in Tennessee by ownership tenure, 2004

Tenure	Ownerships			Sample size
	Number	Standard error	Percent	
years	- - - - thousand - - - -			count
<10	30	11	6.5	16
10–24	194	77	42.3	39
25–49	172	68	37.5	63
50+	8	3	1.7	11
No answer	55	25	12.0	22

The widely varying values and attitudes of family forest landowners are reflected in the reasons they give for owning land. In 2004, aesthetics was chosen by landowners (an estimated 252,000 ownerships) as the most important reason they had for owning forest land, followed by family legacy (226,000), nature protection (201,000), and privacy (187,000) (table 4). Land investment ranked high with an estimated 182,000 family forest landowners. Timber production seemingly took a backseat in importance, although 60,000 owners did indicate that this was an important reason for forest land ownership. However, these categories are not exclusive, meaning that those listing aesthetics as their most important reason for ownership were not necessarily averse to timber harvesting. In fact, many list timber harvest or other forestry activity as a recent event on their land.

According to the NWOS, timber harvests have occurred on an estimated 270,000 of Tennessee's family forest ownerships, with harvest occurring on about 47,000 ownerships during the period 2000–2004 (tables 5 and 6). In 2004, saw-log harvesting occurred on more family-owned forest land ownerships than did pulpwood harvesting or firewood harvesting (table 5). Other activities related to timber management occurring during 2000–2004 include tree planting by an estimated 45,000 ownerships, and the application of chemicals by 49,000 ownerships. Efforts to reduce fire hazards occurred on about 26,000 ownerships during 2000–2004 (table 6). Recreation was another forest activity enjoyed by many of the State's family forest landowners. In 2004, some 192,000 owners listed recreation (public and private) as an activity occurring in the past 5 years on their forest land.

Table 4—Estimated number of family-owned forests in Tennessee by reason for owning forest land, 2004

	Ownerships			
Reason[a]	Number	Standard error	Percent	Sample size
	- - - - thousand - - - -			count
Aesthetics	252	46	55	104
Nature protection	201	43	44	83
Land investment	182	63	40	88
Part of farm, home, or cabin[b]	140	29	31	40
Privacy	187	38	41	33
Family legacy	226	45	49	97
Nontimber forest products	178	36	39	102
Firewood production	33	12	7	21
Timber production	60	22	13	25
Hunting or fishing	50	15	11	46
Other recreation	115	34	25	61
No answer	94	23	20	58

Numbers include landowners who ranked each objective as very important (1) or important (2) on a seven-point Likert scale.

[a] Categories are not exclusive.

[b] Includes primary and secondary residences.

Table 5—Estimated number of family-owned forests in Tennessee by timber harvesting activities, 2004

Activity	Ownerships			Sample size
	Number	Standard error	Percent	
	- - - - thousand - - - -			count
Timber harvest				
Yes	270	68	59	124
No	178	61	39	52
No answer	11	11	2	2
Products harvested[a]				
Saw logs	152	39	33	89
Pulpwood	20	10	4	28
Firewood	66	23	14	36
Other	163	61	36	76
Received professional consultation[b]	53	22	12	37
Recent harvest (within 5 years)	47	13	10	48

[a] Categories are not exclusive.
[b] Most recent harvest.

Table 6—Estimated number of family-owned forests in Tennessee by recent (past 5 years) forestry activity, 2004

Activity[a]	Ownerships			Sample size
	Number	Standard error	Percent	
	- - - - thousand - - - -			count
Timber harvest	47	13	10	48
Collection of NTFPs	60	25	13	25
Site preparation	8	3	2	17
Tree planting	45	28	10	29
Fire hazard reduction	26	12	6	17
Application of chemicals	49	18	11	25
Road/trail maintenance	62	24	14	52
Wildlife habitat improvement	59	24	13	37
Posting land	178	42	39	44
Private recreation	181	48	39	40
Public recreation	11	8	2	4
Cost share	10	9	2	9
Conservation easement[b]	15	10	3	4
Green certification[b]	10	5	2	15

NTFPs = nontimber forest products.
[a] Categories are not exclusive.
[b] Not limited to past 5 years.

A limited number of family forest landowners formally develop a management plan or seek advice in managing their land for timber production, or other forest-related amenities. Only 2 percent of the 459,000 private landowners have a written management plan to help guide their land use decisions (table 7). Although few have a written plan, some 65,000 family forest landowners (14 percent) at least have sought advice about managing their land. Of those, 75 percent (49,000) consulted with experts from the Tennessee Division of Forestry or The University of Tennessee Extension, or from a Federal agency. It is important to note that the estimate of the percent of landowners with a written management plan in 2004 may be much less than is actually the case, because the total number of landowners is used to calculate the percentage and not all landowners in Tennessee are interested in forest land management. The estimate does not provide a clear representation of the population of forest landowners that are actively managing their land with a written management plan and/or having consulted with professional foresters. In addition, the small size of many landholdings (60 percent of landholdings in the State were < 10 acres in size in 2004) makes it impractical for many landowners to actively manage for timber, an activity that generally benefits from the development of management plans and the consultation of forestry professionals.

Table 7—Estimated number of family-owned forests in Tennessee by management plan, advice sought, and advice source, 2004

Activity	Ownerships			
	Number	Standard error	Percent	Sample size
	- - - - thousand - - - -			count
Written management plan				
Yes	11	5	2	18
No	438	89	95	152
No answer	10	6	2	8
Sought advice				
Yes	65	22	14	52
No	394	87	86	125
No answer	0	0	0	1
Advice source[a]				
State forestry agency	34	12	7	32
Extension	4	2	1	8
Other State agency	1	0	0	2
Federal agency	11	7	2	9
Private consultant	13	9	3	14
Forest industry forester	10	9	2	7
Logger	6	3	1	10
Other landowner	3	1	1	6

[a] Categories are not exclusive.

Productive Capacity of Tennessee Forest Ecosystems

Productive capacity refers to the ability of forests to produce goods and services for humans (U.S. Department of Agriculture 2004a). This definition incorporates aspects of both the environmental and economic sustainability of Tennessee's forest systems. Maintaining the productive capacity of the State's forests is essential because people and wildlife in Tennessee rely on a productive, healthy forest to supply livelihoods, wood, wood products, food, fuel, cover, habitat, recreation, and many other goods and services year after year.

FIA defines timberland as any forested land that is available for timber production; that is, forested land not withdrawn from timber harvesting by law. A good example of forest land withdrawn from timber harvesting by law in Tennessee is the Great Smoky Mountains National Park. Thus, timberland is the land base from which Tennessee citizens can obtain multiple timber and nontimber products and services. The timberland base in Tennessee should remain productive. In Tennessee, timberland area and forest land area followed similar trends from 1961 to 2004 (fig. 32). Although forest land remained relatively unchanged

between 1999 and 2004, Tennessee lost productive timberland during the same time period. Timberland declined an estimated 205,000 acres during 1999–2004 and declined about 178,000 acres from 1961 to 2004. From 1999 to 2004, forest land remained stable while timberland declined because the estimate of reserved forest land increased. Because reserved forest land represents a small component of all forest land, especially at the unit scale, slight increases may represent statistical noise in the data rather than real change.

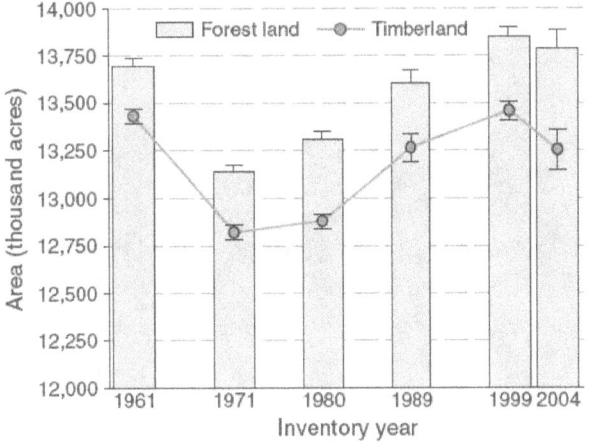

Figure 32—Forest land and timberland acreage in Tennessee, 1961–2004. Error bars represent one standard error.

A natural pine stand that has been marked for harvest.

29

Composition of Tennessee Timberlands

The oak-hickory forest-type group accounted for an estimated 74 percent (9.9 million acres) of the timberland in Tennessee in 2004 (fig. 33). The loblolly-shortleaf pine type group accounted for

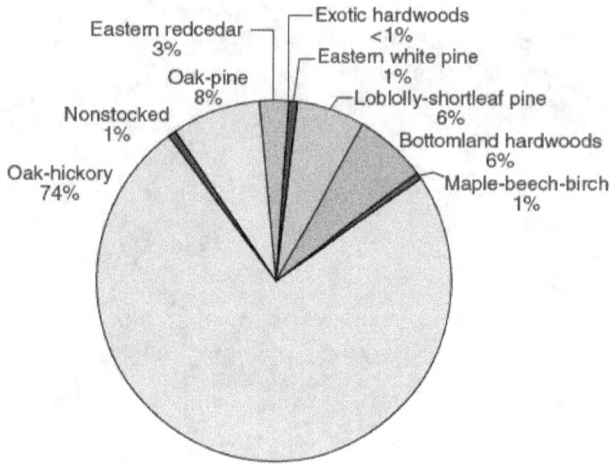

Figure 33—Percent of timberland by forest-type group, Tennessee, 2004.

only 6 percent, the majority of which (302,000 acres) is located in the eastern part of the State. Mixed stands of the oak-pine type accounted for an estimated 8 percent of timberland in Tennessee. Bottomland hardwoods (elm-ash-cottonwood and oak-gum-cypress types), in west Tennessee, accounted for about 6 percent of the timberland. The eastern redcedar type accounted for an estimated 3 percent of timberland and was located predominantly in Central Tennessee (224,000 of 351,000 total estimated acres).

Between 1999 and 2004, the only significant changes in composition were a loss of an estimated 225,000 acres of the loblolly-shortleaf pine type and a gain of about 234,000 acres of oak-hickory (fig. 34). These changes may have resulted from the disturbance to Tennessee's southern yellow pine forests caused by the SPB outbreak of 1999–2002. Recent anecdotal evidence suggests that many of the impacted stands appear to be shifting to hardwood dominance due to, usually, the existence of hardwood regeneration in the understory.

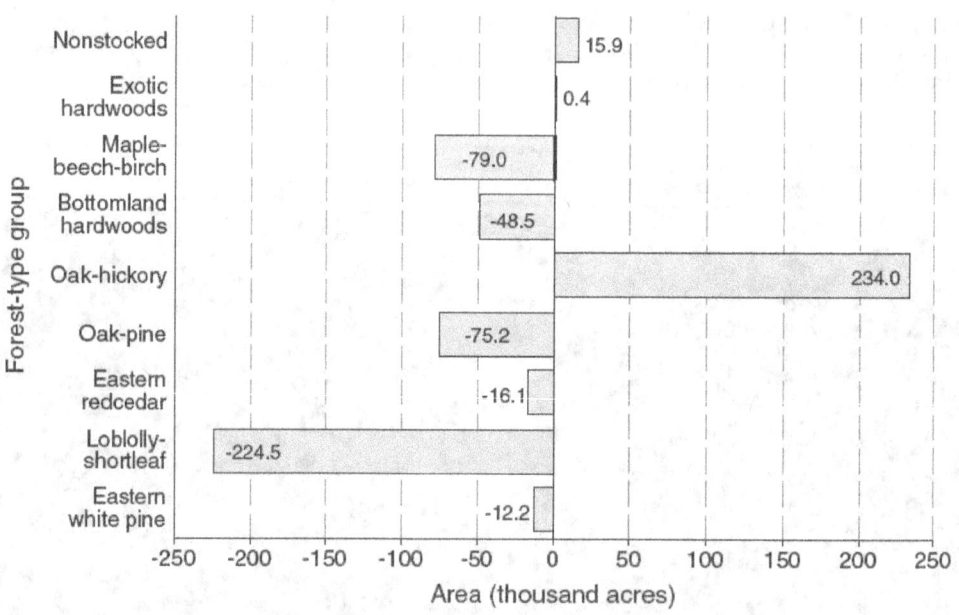

Figure 34—Changes in composition of timberland in Tennessee, 1999–2004.

Standing Volume on Timberland

The standing volume of growing stock on timberland in Tennessee increased about 36 percent between 1989 and 2004. That is an average increase in volume of around 2 percent per year. In 1989, there was an estimated 16.6 billion cubic feet of growing-stock volume standing on Tennessee's timberland. In 1999, there was an estimated 21.8 billion cubic feet of volume, and in 2004 there was an estimated 22.6 billion cubic feet of volume. The average diameter of many trees in Tennessee's forests were getting larger during the period 1989–2004, as indicated by the distribution of volume among diameter classes shifting to larger diameters. In 1989, the diameter class with the greatest volume was 9.0–10.9 inches. Growing-stock volume was greatest in the 11.0–12.9 inches diameter class in 1999 and greatest in the 13.0–14.9 inches diameter class in 2004 (fig. 35).

In 2004, yellow-poplar was the most numerous growing-stock tree species on Tennessee timberland (fig. 36), accounting for about 10 percent of all growing-stock trees. However, all oak species combined accounted for an estimated 20 percent of all growing-stock trees in 2004. Species of the loblolly and shortleaf pine group, one of the largest softwood groups in terms of area, simultaneously accounted for an estimated 6 percent of growing-stock trees.

In 2004, the forested stands on Tennessee's timberlands were predominantly of natural origin. Consistently, between 1989 and 2004, about 96 percent of timberland area

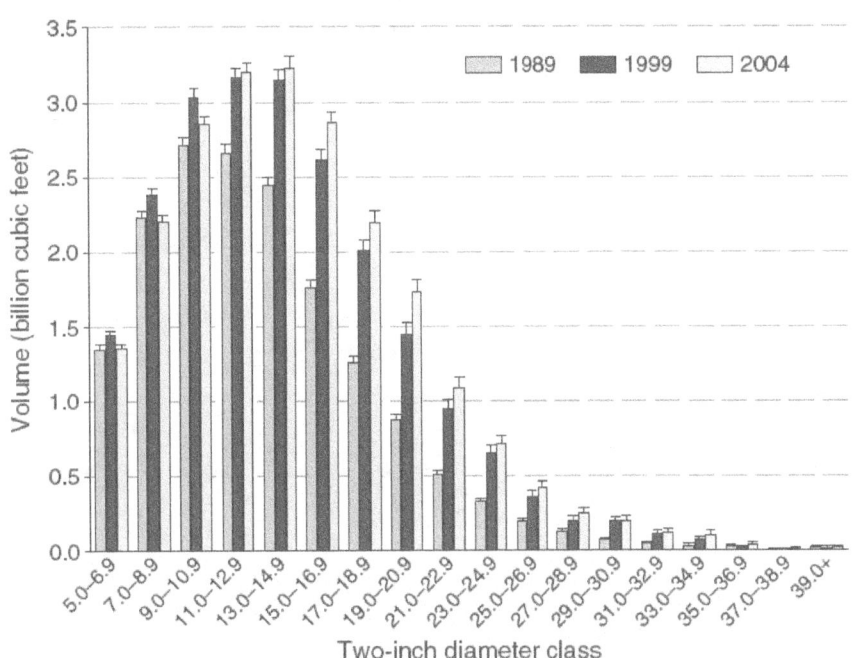

Figure 35—Volume of growing stock on timberland for each 2-inch diameter class in Tennessee for 1989, 1999, and 2004. Error bars represent one standard error.

Mixed hardwood forests are very common in Tennessee. The closest leaves are that of a member of the hickory (*Carya*) genus.

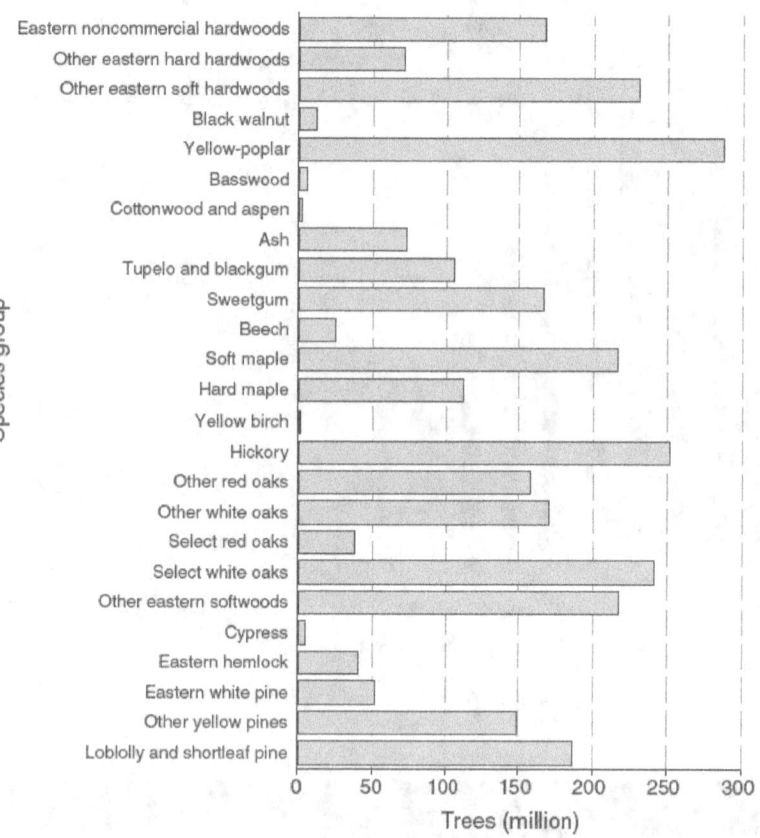

Figure 36—Number of growing-stock trees on timberland by species group in Tennessee, 2004.

originated naturally (was not planted) (fig. 37). In 2004, planted stands accounted for an estimated 497,000 acres of timberland across the State (fig. 38). The majority (29 percent or 146,000 acres) of the planted area was in West Central Tennessee (fig. 38). The Central unit (4 percent of all planted area) had the smallest area in planted stands in Tennessee, and the East unit (17 percent of all planted area) had the second smallest area in planted stands.

In 2004, about 96 percent of the acreage in planted stands in Tennessee was originally planted with loblolly pine (i.e., loblolly pine was the dominant planted species). Due to natural succession along with various levels of management intensity and in some cases plantation abandonment, not all of that acreage remained as a loblolly-shortleaf pine forest type as of 2004. According to the results of the 2004 inventory, only 66 percent of planted stands are classified as belonging to the loblolly-shortleaf pine forest-type group.

A white oak (Quercus alba) leaf that is one of countless that covers the forest floor in winter.

In Tennessee, the stands with clear evidence of planting in 2004 belonged to one of five forest-type groups (fig. 39): (1) white-red-jack pine, (2) loblolly-shortleaf pine, (3) pinyon-juniper (eastern redcedar), (4) oak-pine, or (5) oak-hickory. Percentage of area in planted stands within a forest-type group was greatest for the loblolly-shortleaf pine type group (39 percent of all area within the loblolly-shortleaf pine type group was planted) and second greatest for the oak-pine forest-type group (11 percent). Planted oak-hickory stands accounted for < 1 percent of the area in the oak-hickory forest-type group (fig. 39).

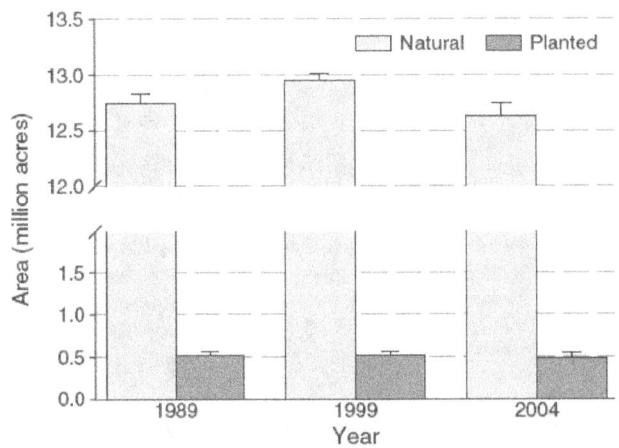

Figure 37—Area of timberland by stand origin, Tennessee, 2004. Error bars represent one standard error.

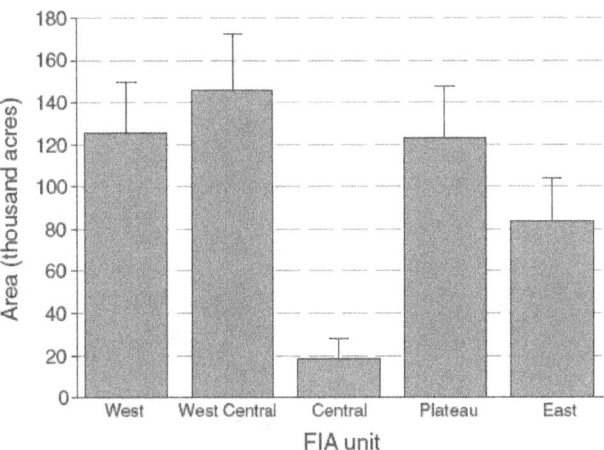

Figure 38—Area of timberland with a planted stand origin for FIA units in Tennessee, 2004. Error bars represent one standard error.

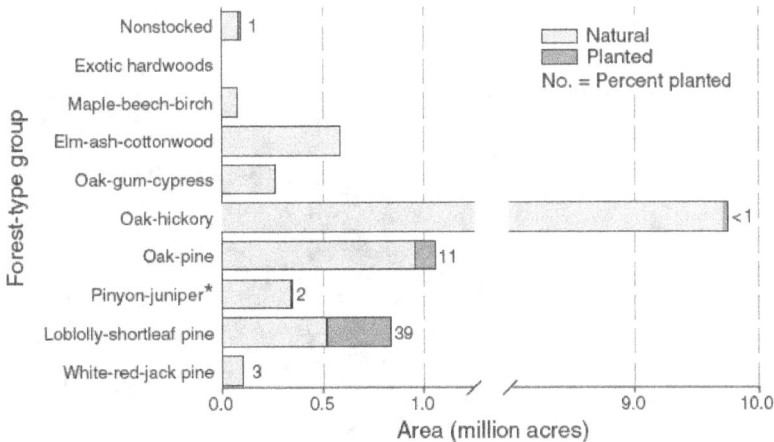

Figure 39—Area of timberland in each forest-type group by stand origin, Tennessee, 2004. *Consists primarily of eastern red cedar.

A Note about Tree Quality

Tree grade is a classification that indicates the suitability of individual sawtimber-size trees to yield factory grade lumber or construction strength timbers. Factory grade lumber is used in furniture, flooring, pallets, and other products. Unlike log grade, tree grade applies to the whole tree and is generally evaluated before the tree is felled. FIA adapted the hardwood tree grading system devised by Hanks (1976). The FIA system is based on the amount and distribution of surface defects, the amount of rotten wood, and the location of the utilizable log or logs within the tree.

In the 2004 Tennessee inventory, each sawtimber-size, growing-stock hardwood tree was assigned a tree grade of 1–5. Trees suitable for factory lumber were graded 1–3, with grade 1 being the best and grade 3 the lowest quality. Grade 4 trees have too many defects to yield factory lumber but can yield construction timbers or railroad ties. Tree grade 5 indicates that the utilizable material is in the upper stem, too high above the

ground for evaluation by field crews. While most of the tree data collected by FIA are quantitative measurements (e.g., diameter and tree height), tree grade is qualitative and somewhat subjective in nature. In fact, in a recent investigation Zarnoch and Turner (2005) found that FIA tree grade classifications made in the field in Kentucky often overestimated grade 1 trees.

Overall, for all live trees that are of gradable standards, tree grade declined from 1999 to 2004. For instance, in 1999 about 10 percent of the gradable trees were classified as grade 1, while 21 percent and 57 percent of trees were classified as grades 2 and 3, respectively. In 1999, 12 percent of gradable size trees did not meet the requirements for grades 1, 2, or 3 (i.e., they were below-grade). In 2004, the percentage of below-grade trees increased to 15 percent and grade 1 trees decreased to 7 percent.

The trends for hardwood trees only mirrored those for hardwoods and softwoods combined. Below-grade trees increased from 15 to 18 percent from

A high-quality stand of cherrybark oak (*Quercus falcata* var. *pagodifolia*), common in the western portion of Tennessee.

1999 to 2004. Grade 1 hardwood trees declined from 10 to 7 percent over the same period. The percentages of hardwood trees of gradable size that were classified as grade 2 or grade 3 remained at about 23 percent and 53 percent, respectively.

Annual Growth, Removals, and Mortality

The estimate of average annual net growth for all species increased from about 843 million cubic feet during the period between 1989 and 1998 to about 848 million cubic feet during the period between 1999 and 2004 (fig. 40). Hardwood average annual net growth increased from about 690 million cubic feet to about 809 million cubic feet over the same time periods, whereas average annual softwood net growth decreased from 154 million to 38 million cubic feet. The decrease in softwood growth appears to have been driven by the SPB outbreak of 1999–2002. Net growth-to-removal ratios remained positive for hardwoods (1.8 million cubic feet of growth for every 1 million cubic feet removed) and became negative for softwoods between 1999 and 2004, again most likely due to the same SPB outbreak. Average annual mortality, while remaining about level for hardwoods, increased for softwoods in the State for the period between 1999 and 2004. In addition, removals and mortality remained a very small portion of the total volume of all live trees during 1999–2004 (fig. 41).

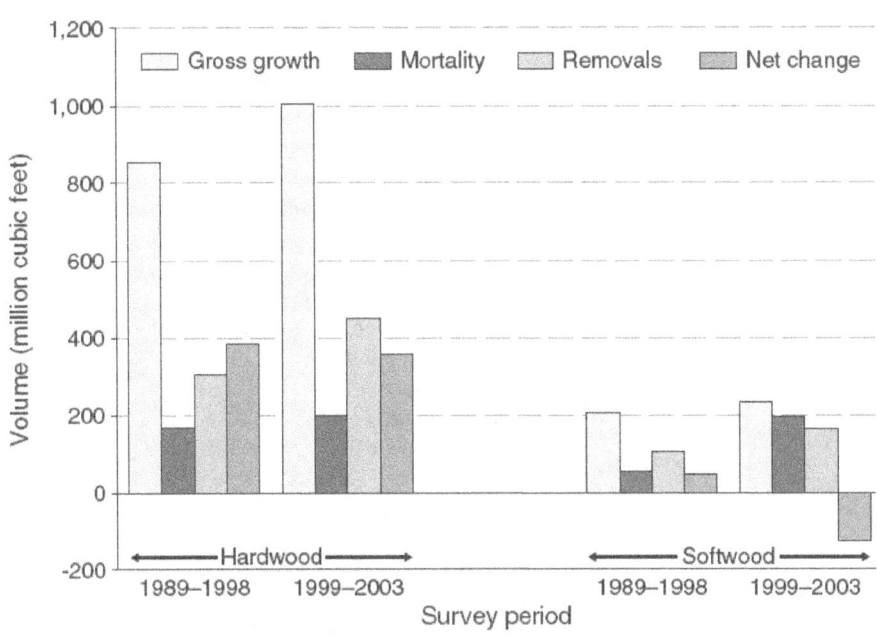

Figure 40—Average annual gross growth, mortality, removals, and net change of all live trees on timberland in Tennessee, 1989–1998, and 1999–2003. Net growth = gross growth - mortality.

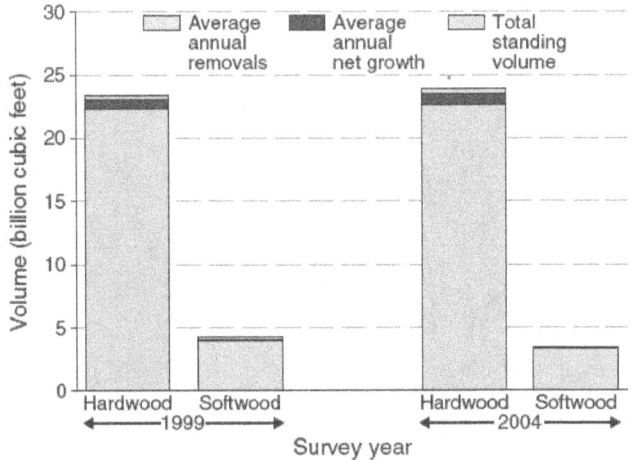

Figure 41—Average annual removals, growth, and total volume of all live trees on timberland in Tennessee, 1999 and 2004.

Forest Management Types in Tennessee

Active and passive management of Tennessee timberlands helps create a diversity of products and social and ecological values that are important to citizens of and visitors to Tennessee, in addition to diverse habitat types for wildlife. It is important to characterize our forests in a way that helps people understand what kinds of benefits the forests can provide. By characterizing the timberland in Tennessee by management type, whether actively managed or not, we can provide a clearer picture of the types of forests that are working for Tennessee.

Timberland was classified into one of six forest management types according to stocking and stand origin. The forest management types are pine plantation, natural pine, oak-pine, upland hardwood, lowland hardwood, and nonstocked.

Statewide, the area classified as pine plantation declined by an estimated 83,000 acres from 1999 to 2004 (fig. 42).

In 2004, an estimated 334,000 acres of Tennessee timberland was managed as pine plantations. However, this acreage was not evenly distributed across the State. Pine plantation acreage accounted for about 5 percent of timberland in the West unit, 4 percent in the West Central unit, 3 percent in the Plateau unit, and 2 percent in the East unit (fig. 43). Pine plantations accounted for < 1 percent of timberland area in the Central unit of the State. The highest proportion of the State's pine plantation acreage is located in the West (29 percent) and West Central (26 percent) units. This ratio was 25 percent and 17 percent in the Plateau and East units, respectively. Statewide, stands of natural pine declined 169,000 acres between 1999 and 2004, but in 2004 they still covered almost three times as much area as pine plantations (fig. 42). Similarly, the area classified as oak-pine declined an estimated 75,000 acres between 1999 and 2004. Observed declines in area covered by pine plantations and natural pine and oak-pine stands may be explained by the mortality caused by the SPB epidemic that occurred between the 1999 and 2004 inventories. As

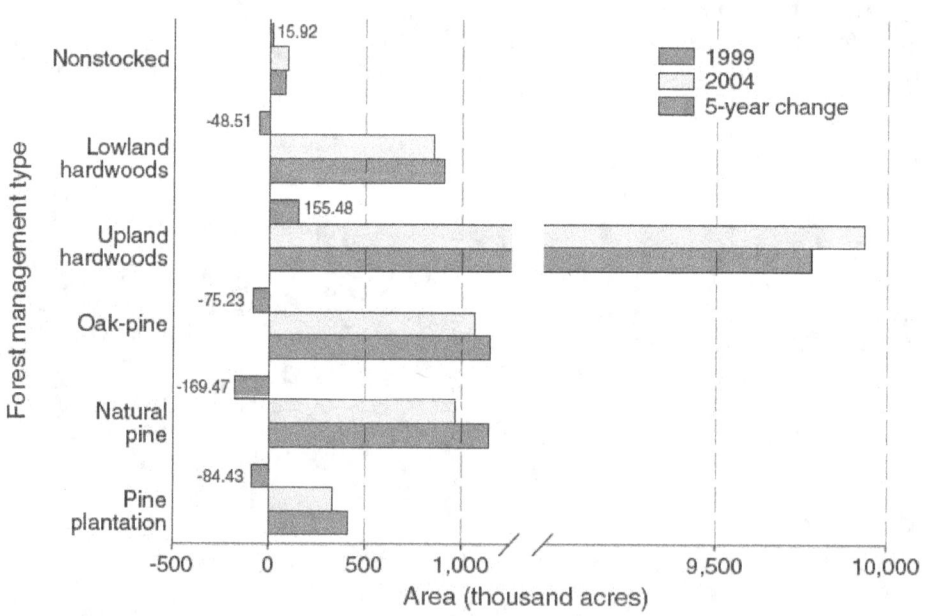

Figure 42—Timberland area by classified forest management type for 1999 and 2004, and 5-year change, for Tennessee.

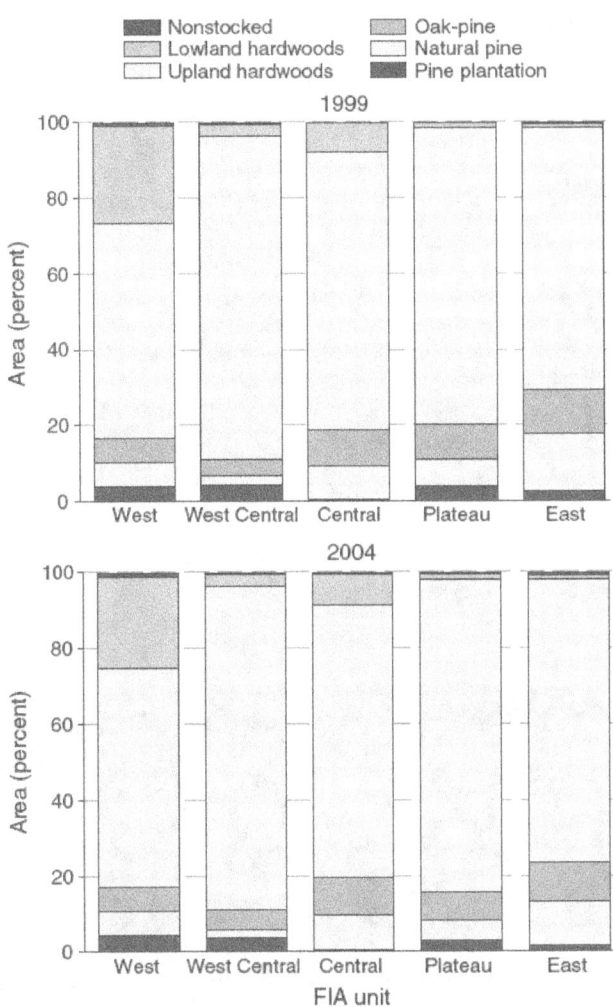

Legend:
- Nonstocked
- Lowland hardwoods
- Upland hardwoods
- Oak-pine
- Natural pine
- Pine plantation

1999

2004

FIA unit

Figure 43—Percent of timberland area for each FIA unit in Tennessee by forest management type, 1999 and 2004.

Figure 44—Advance hardwood regeneration, mostly sclerophyllous oak species, growing within a pine stand partially killed by southern pine beetle activity. Horsehitch Gap, TN.

of 2004, much of the area impacted by SPB appeared to have quickly recovered because many stands contained advance hardwood regeneration in the understory (fig. 44).

In 2004, more than 80 percent of timberland in Tennessee was classified as either upland or lowland hardwoods. However, between 1999 and 2004 the area covered by lowland hardwoods declined while area covered by upland hardwoods increased (fig. 42). Lowland hardwoods declined an estimated 49,000 acres. Upland hardwoods increased by about 155,000 acres. Lowland hardwood declines were primarily in the western part of the State, while increases in upland hardwoods were primarily in the eastern part of the State (fig. 43). Many of the acres that contributed to increases in the upland hardwood management type could be a result of the decline in the pine management types as a result of the SPB.

In Tennessee, stands in the pine plantation management type were generally much younger than those in the other management types in 2004. For example, in 2004, about 68 percent of the acreage in pine plantations was in stands that were 20 years old or younger (fig. 45). This is a change from 1999 when only 51 percent of pine plantations were in stands that were 20 years old or younger. The oldest pine plantation recorded in 1999 was between 61 and 70 years of age. In 2004 the oldest pine plantation was between 51 and 60 years old (fig. 45). It appears that removals

and mortality were heaviest for the older stands in the pine plantation management type during 1999–2004.

In 2004, the upland hardwood management type contained some of the oldest stands observed in the State, with an estimated 16,000 acres in the 121+ age class (fig. 45). In both the upland hardwood and lowland hardwood management types, acreage in age classes 51–60 years and above generally increased between 1999 and 2004, while acreage in the younger age classes generally declined during that period (fig. 45). This trend is consistent with other estimates, such as the shift of the overall diameter distribution to larger diameters, which signify an ageing forest resource. Tennessee's forests are getting older.

Mature hardwood forest in west Tennessee.

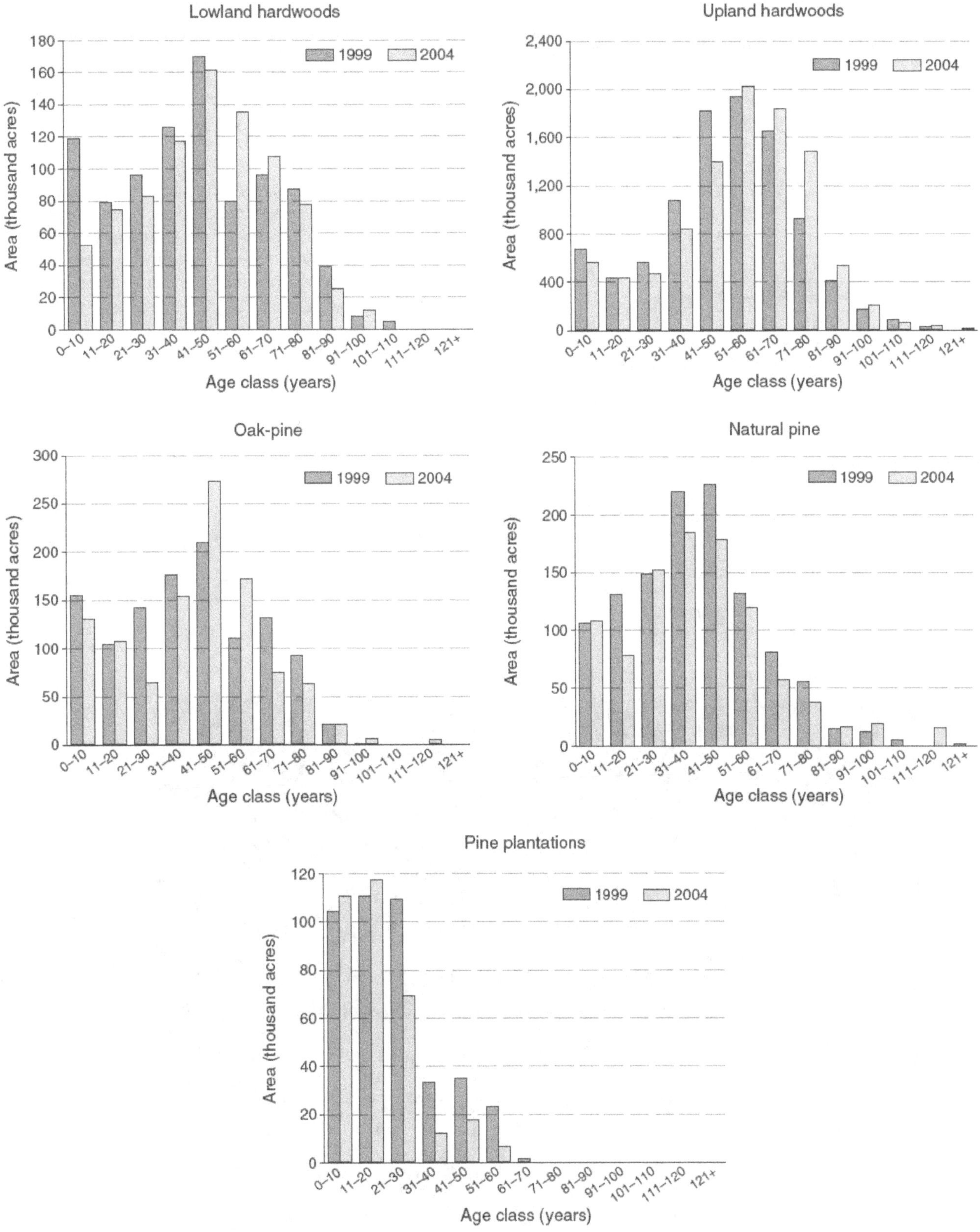

Figure 45—Age-class distributions for each forest management type in Tennessee, 1999 and 2004.

Forest Stand Treatments

Tree cutting occurred on an estimated 1.1 million acres (8 percent) of Tennessee timberland between 1999 and 2004 (fig. 46). Tree cutting was identified as the

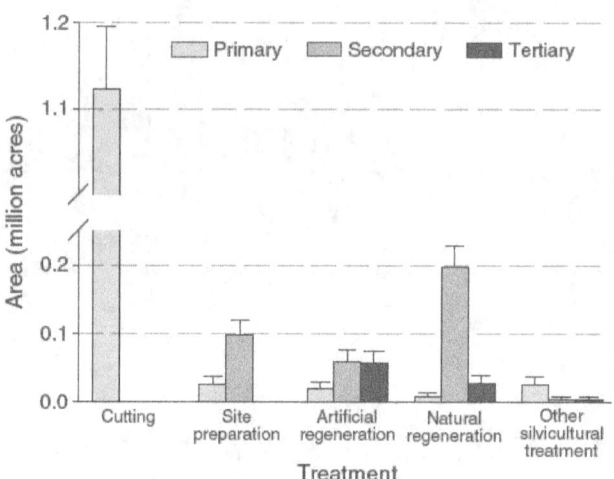

Figure 46—Area of timberland disturbed by disturbance category and ordinal classification, Tennessee, 2004. Error bars represent one standard error.

primary treatment in all cases of observed stand treatments on FIA plots. Secondary and tertiary treatments are treatments that are additional to a primary treatment. For example, following cutting, an area can be site prepared (secondary treatment) and then planted (tertiary treatment). In that case, the observed plot contributes to estimates in all three categories. Thus, the primary, secondary, and tertiary treatments are not mutually exclusive across categories (fig. 46), however, they are mutually exclusive within a treatment. A plot can receive multiple treatments, as when cutting (primary) is followed by site preparation (secondary) and artificial regeneration (tertiary), but an individual treatment (such as cutting) cannot be both a primary and secondary treatment.

Natural regeneration was the dominant type of regeneration on Tennessee timberland in 2004 (fig. 46). An estimated 30,000 acres Statewide were planted annually between 1999 and 2004 (fig. 47). The

Planted cherrybark oak (*Quercus falcata* var. *pagodifolia*) near Carthage, Tennessee.

greatest planting activity occurred in the West Central unit. The West, Central, Plateau, and East units had similar levels of annual artificial regeneration. While pine plantations and other forms of artificial regeneration continued to play an important role on the Tennessee landscape, they accounted for only a fraction of timberland in the State.

The majority of tree cutting activity on FIA plots is categorized as final harvest, partial harvest, or seed-tree/shelterwood harvest. A final harvest is the removal of the majority of the merchantable trees in a stand, leaving a residual stocking of < 50 percent. A partial harvest is defined as the removal of primarily the highest quality trees but can include some uneven-aged silvicultural methods such as group selection. The seed-tree/shelterwood category captures stands that are harvested in which seed trees or shelterwood trees remain in the residual stand.

A final harvest occurred on an estimated 79,000 acres of timberland annually between 1999 and 2004 (fig. 47). About 33 percent (26,000 acres) of annual final harvests were recorded in the Plateau unit. The least amount of final harvest cutting occurred in the Central unit. Partial harvests were highest (52,000 acres) for the Plateau unit. Seed-tree/shelterwood harvests were rare throughout the State (fig. 47). Readers should be advised that the treatment categories discussed here are assigned based on observations made at each plot. Multiple years may pass between the actual treatment and the determinations made by field crews, so the determinations are therefore somewhat subjective. Comparisons with previous estimates should be made with caution.

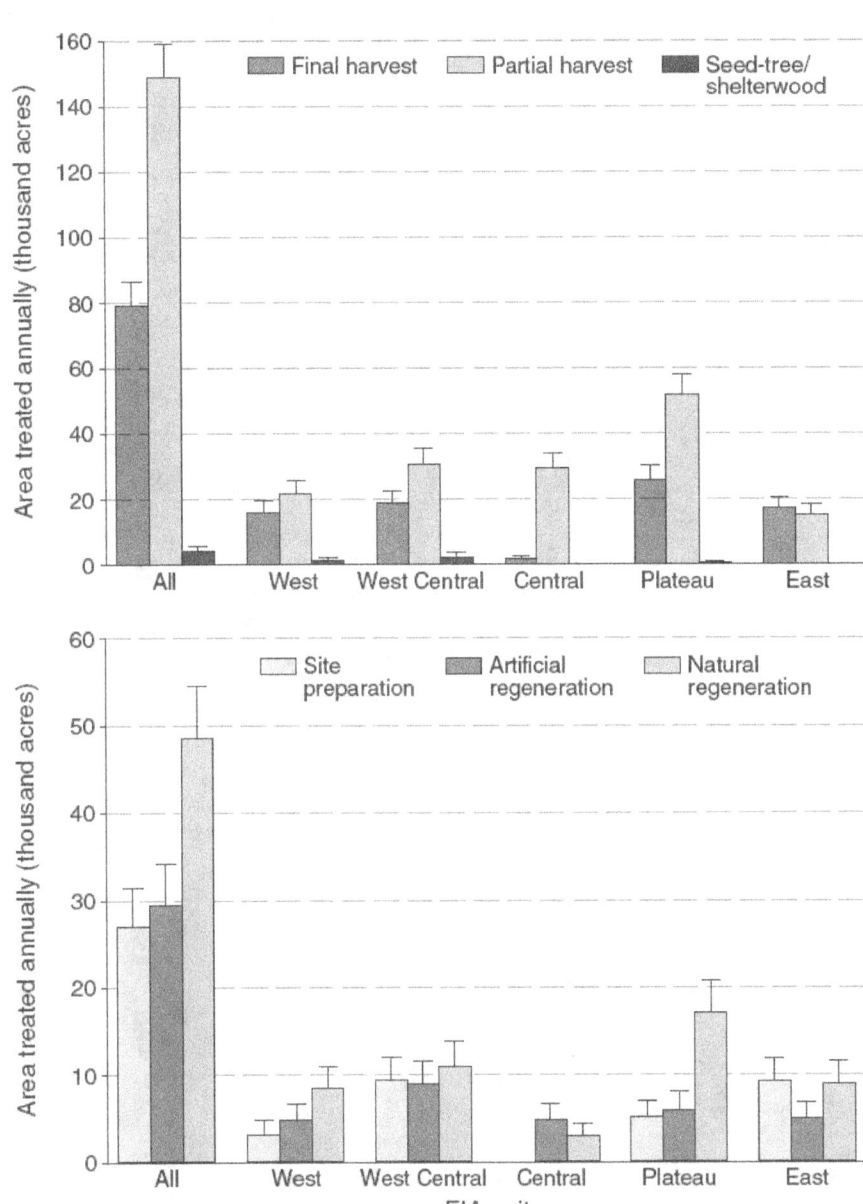

Figure 47—Timberland area treated annually by treatment category, Tennessee, 1999–2004. Error bars represent one standard error.

Major Threats to Tennessee Forest Ecosystems

Numerous threats to the sustainability of Tennessee's forests exist, including increasing numbers and frequency of nonnative invasive plant species, increasing landscape fragmentation or loss of open (undeveloped) space, and increased levels of ozone in the atmosphere to name only a few.

Invasive Plant Species

Invasive species are a growing problem in southern forests. Invasive plants have the potential to change the ecological characteristics of a site, including modifying soil properties and outcompeting native species. The overall result can include reduced density and diversity of native woody regeneration (Oswalt and others 2007) which can impact the ecological and economic trajectories of forest stands.

Tennessee, along with other southern States, began collecting information on the presence and cover of invasive species

on all forested plots in 2001. Each of these plots is composed of four subplots. The data presented here were collected on 9,680 subplots between 2001 and 2004. Data are summarized by subplot.

Thirty-two percent of all forested subplots and 52 percent of all sampled forested plots contained at least one nonnative invasive plant species. Japanese honeysuckle (*Lonicera japonica*) was the most frequently observed species, and occurred on 24 percent of all forested subplots (2,322 subplots) and 76 percent of all forested subplots containing at least one nonnative invasive species (fig. 48). Nepalese browntop (*Microstegium vimineum*) was the second most common nonnative invasive on sampled subplots. Both species persist under full canopy cover. The most frequently observed nonnative invasive tree species was tree-of-heaven (*Ailanthus altissima*), which occurred on 195 forested subplots (6 percent) (fig. 48). Privets (Japanese and Chinese) were also found on numerous subplots (fig. 48). Privets, when combined, were observed on more

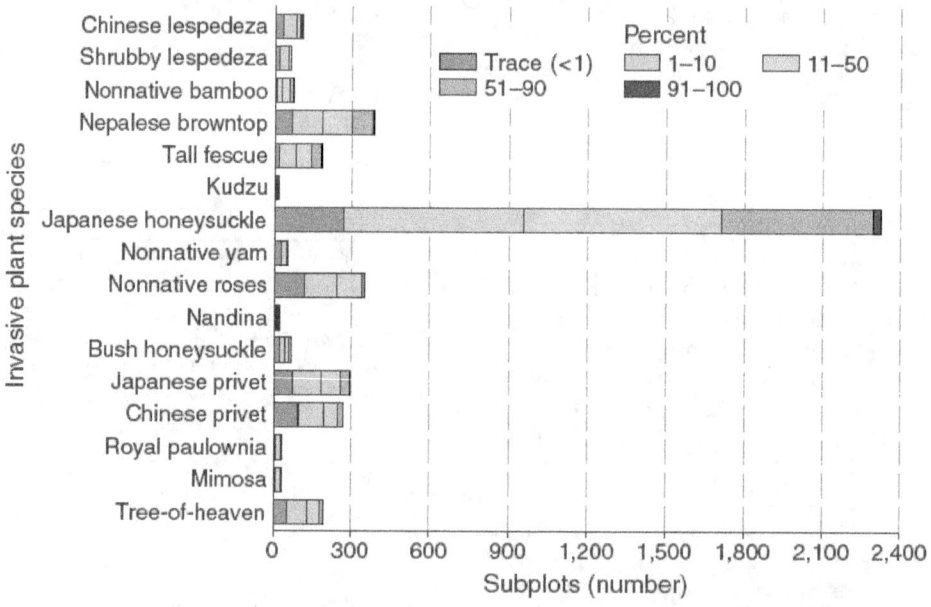

Figure 48—Number of forested subplots sampled that contained at least one nonnative invasive plant species by nonnative plant species present, Tennessee, 2004. Bar color represents understory coverage of the nonnative plant.

A nonnative grass imported from Asia, *Microstegium vimineum*, can quickly colonize a disturbed forest and can cause significant harm to the natural flora.

forested subplots than any of the other sampled nonnative invasive plants with the exception of honeysuckle.

Landscape Fragmentation—Loss of Undeveloped Space

Human-mediated development is a major force changing the forests of Tennessee, the forests of the United States, and global forest resources. In most cases the impact of human development on natural resources is negative. Replacement of productive forest land with impervious surfaces and forest fragmentation through changing land use from forest to nonforest conditions are two of the primary components of the loss of undeveloped space.

An analysis of the 2001 NLCD (Riitters and others 2002) revealed that about 54 percent of the Tennessee landscape was in

some type of forest (edge, patch, or interior; see Riitters and others 2002 for detailed explanation) (fig. 49). The NLCD analysis is consistent with the FIA plot-based estimate of about 52 percent forest cover. The largest

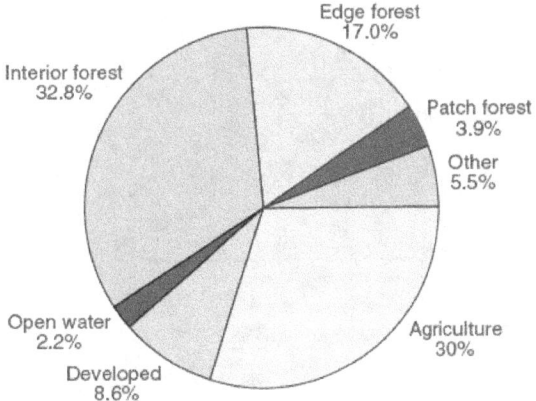

Figure 49—Percent of Tennessee landscape classified according to seven land use categories, 2001. Adapted from a moving window analysis (see Riitters and others 2002) of the 2001 National Land Cover Data.

portion (32.8 percent) of the Tennessee landscape was covered by interior forests. Edge forests covered an estimated 17 percent of Tennessee's landscape, and patch forests (small patches of intact forests not large enough to be called interior forest) accounted for an estimated 3.9 percent. The most heavily forested units in Tennessee were the West Central and Plateau units. Moreover, interior forests dominated the West Central and Plateau units (fig. 50).

Agriculture, which was most extensive in western Tennessee (fig. 51), accounted for about 30 percent of land Statewide (fig. 49). Proportionally, agricultural land cover was lowest in the West Central and Plateau units, where forests dominated (figs. 50 and 51). The Central unit, with an estimated 36 percent of land in agricultural cover, had the second largest proportion of agriculture for all of the FIA units.

Developed space was concentrated around the major cities in the State (fig. 50) and along corridors created by the vast interstate and highway system across the State. It is easy to see the path of the major roads in Tennessee by looking for strings of

developed space (red pixels in fig. 50) on the fragmentation map. For example, one can easily follow the path of Highway 51, paralleling the Mississippi River in West Tennessee, and the path of Interstate 75 can be seen in East Tennessee. This, of course, is no surprise because an increase in the development of roads generally corresponds with the loss of undeveloped space. What causes concern is that road miles in Tennessee appear to have increased at an exponential rate during the period 1994–2005 (fig. 52).

Ozone and Tennessee's Forests

Ozone (O_3) is a chemical compound that occurs naturally in the Earth's atmosphere. In the upper atmosphere, ozone is essential for protecting the Earth's surface from intense ultraviolet rays coming from the Sun. In the troposphere, however, ozone becomes a secondary pollutant, contributing to permanent damage to human respiratory systems. Tropospheric ozone also affects the growth and development of forest vegetation (Skelly 2000).

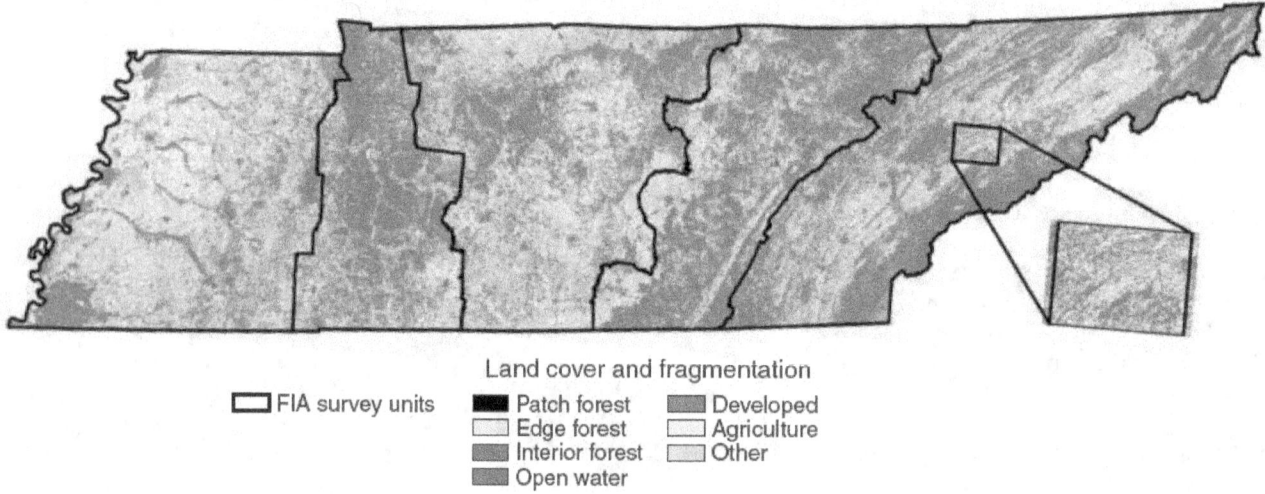

Land cover and fragmentation

☐ FIA survey units   ■ Patch forest   ■ Developed
☐ Edge forest   ☐ Agriculture
■ Interior forest   ☐ Other
■ Open water

Figure 50—Landscape classification of land use in Tennessee according to seven land-use categories. Adapted from a moving window analysis (see Riitters and others 2002) of the 2001 National Land Cover Data.

Nitrogen oxides (NOX) are byproducts of organic fuel combustion and may be particularly high near industrial areas. Volatile organic compounds (VOCs) are emitted from many natural sources such as trees. Chemical compounds in these two groups combine in the presence of sunlight to form tropospheric ozone. Tropospheric ozone concentrations fluctuate naturally in response to weather events and changes in the chemistry of the air. Hot, cloudless summer days produce perfect weather conditions for the chemical reactions that combine NOX and VOCs into harmful ozone.

Pollution due to high concentrations of tropospheric ozone affects forest vegetation growth and directly damages the foliage of sensitive species (Lefohn and others 1997, Coulston and others 2003). Forests in the Eastern United States may be particularly susceptible because of lingering high-pressure systems common in the region, combined with concentrated areas of urbanization and industrialization that generate the precursors to ozone (Skelly 2000). The resulting ozone travels downwind of these population centers, often reaching peak concentrations in remote areas.

High amounts of ozone in the troposphere may result in visible damage to forest vegetation. Some species are known to be particularly sensitive to ozone, and exhibit this sensitivity through changes in leaf pigmentation, leaf senescence, or other species-specific symptoms. These sensitive species are used as bioindicators of ozone presence, and are particularly useful in

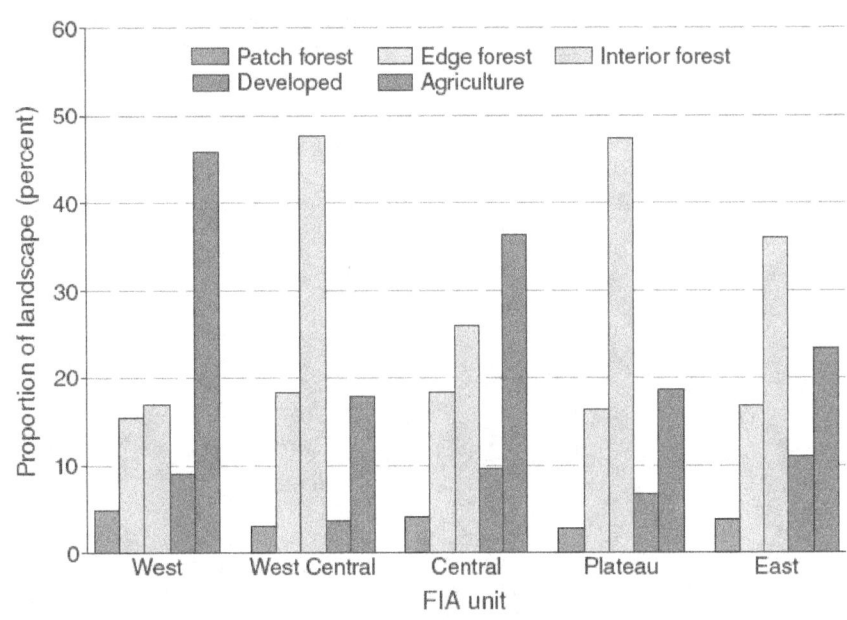

Figure 51—Proportional allocation of land by land use and FIA unit according to five land use categories. Adapted from a moving window analysis (see Riitters and others 2002) of the 2001 National Land Cover Data.

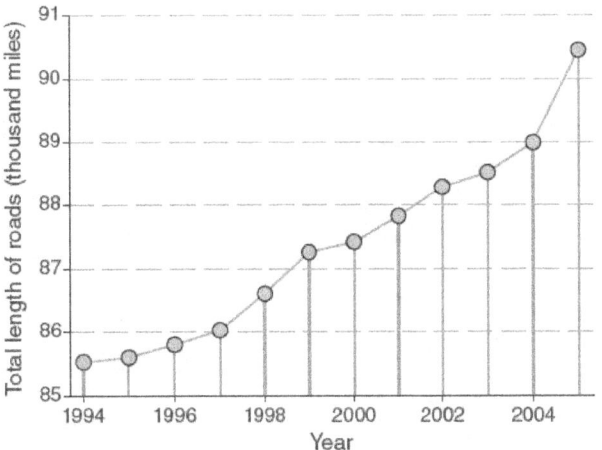

Figure 52—Total linear road miles in Tennessee, 1994–2005. Data from the U.S. Department of Transportation, Federal Highway Administration.

areas where ozone monitoring stations may not be present, such as remote forest locations (Skelly 2000). In Tennessee, species used as bioindicators include black cherry, sassafras, and yellow-poplar, among others (table 8).

Ozone data was collected on 13,687 plants of 7 species from the bioindicator list in Tennessee on a total of 171 sites from 2001 through 2004. Twenty-two percent of all evaluated biosites contained plants that exhibited ozone-related damage. About 2 percent of the plants sampled exhibited signs of ozone-related damage (table 9; see Smith and others 2007 for a detailed description of ozone data collection methods).

Data from the U.S. Environmental Protection Agency (EPA) combined with FIA data suggest that while mean ambient ozone concentrations were in the moderate range during 2000–2004 (fig. 53), the overall impacts of air quality on sensitive species were less severe in Tennessee than in surrounding States (fig. 54).

Table 8—List of bioindicators for Tennessee

Common name	Scientific name
Blackberry	Rubus allegheniensis
Black cherry	Prunus serotina
Milkweed	Asclepias spp.
Yellow-poplar	Liriodendron tulipifera
White ash	Fraxinus americana
Sassafras	Sassafras albidum
Spreading dogbane	Apocynum androsaemifolium
Big leaf aster	Aster macrophylum
Sweetgum	Liquidambar styraciflua
Pin cherry	P. pensylvanica

Table 9—Summary of biosite data, Tennessee, 2001 through 2004

Parameter[a]	Tennessee biomonitoring program				
	2001	2002	2003	2004	Total
Number of biosites evaluated	55	39	37	40	171
Number of biosites with injury	12	7	13	5	37
Number of plants evaluated	2,737	3,295	3,666	3,989	13,687
Number of plants injured	87	101	114	12	314
Average biosite injury score[a]	4.64	2.79	2.39	0.28	—
			number		
Species[b]					
Sweetgum	500 (21)	330 (31)	535 (6)	622 (5)	1,987 (63)
Yellow-poplar	488 (13)	668 (6)	722 (27)	759 (3)	2,637 (49)
Milkweed	207 (0)	71 (13)	120 (0)	177 (0)	575 (13)
Black cherry	237 (0)	574 (0)	641 (1)	448 (0)	1,900 (1)
Blackberry	1,032 (52)	946 (51)	890 (78)	1,181 (4)	4,049 (185)
White ash	112 (1)	257 (0)	204 (2)	202 (0)	775 (3)
Sassafras	161 (0)	449 (0)	554 (0)	600 (0)	1,764 (0)

[a] The biosite index is based on the average injury score (amount * severity) for each species averaged across all species on the biosite multiplied by 1,000.

[b] Total number of injured plants given in parenthesis.

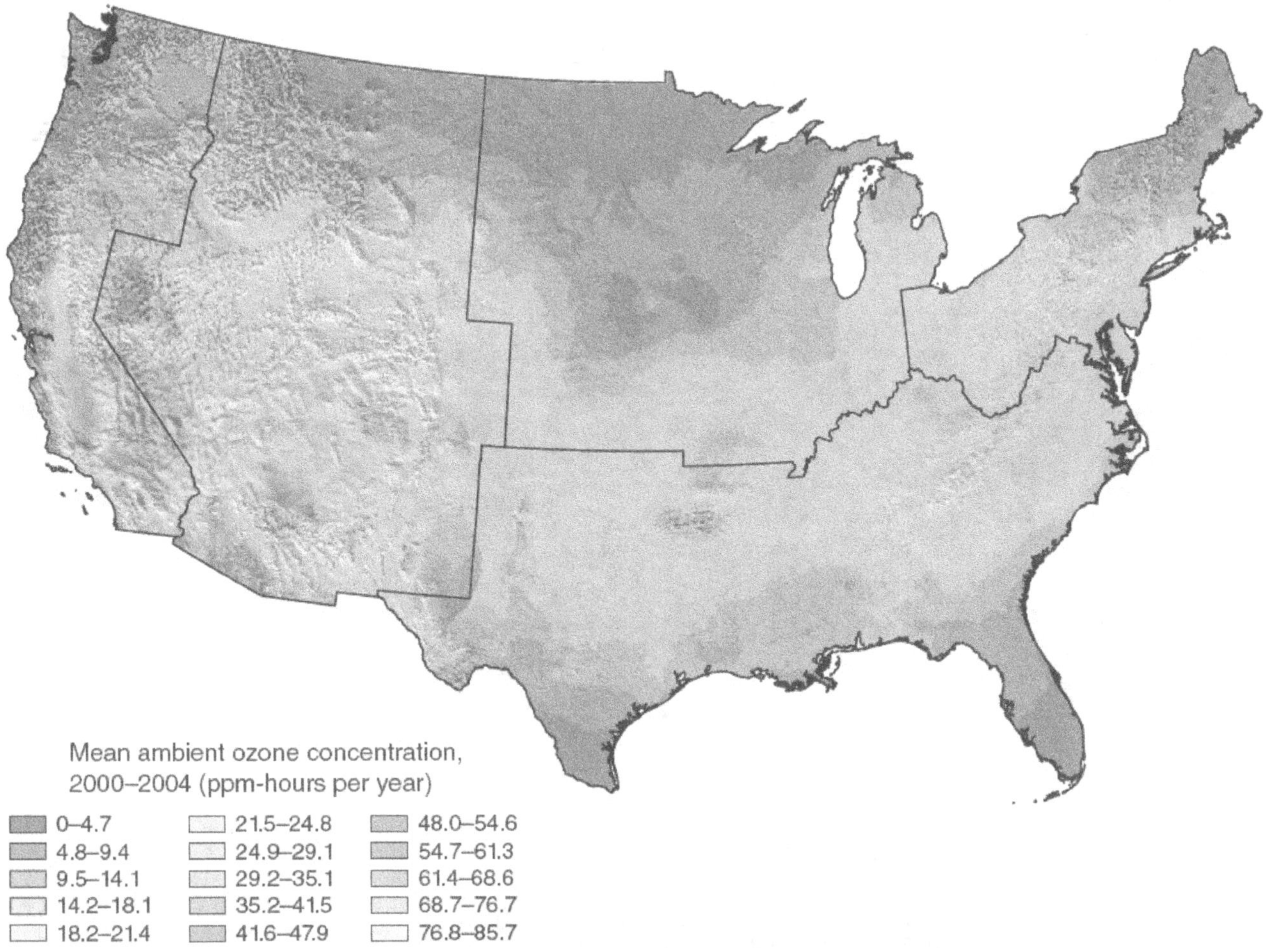

Mean ambient ozone concentration,
2000–2004 (ppm-hours per year)

0–4.7	21.5–24.8	48.0–54.6
4.8–9.4	24.9–29.1	54.7–61.3
9.5–14.1	29.2–35.1	61.4–68.6
14.2–18.1	35.2–41.5	68.7–76.7
18.2–21.4	41.6–47.9	76.8–85.7

Figure 53—Mean ambient ozone concentrations, 2000–2004. (Source: U.S. Environmental Protection Agency)

Sassafras (*Sassafras albidum*) is one of many hardwood tree species that are found growing in Tennessee forests.

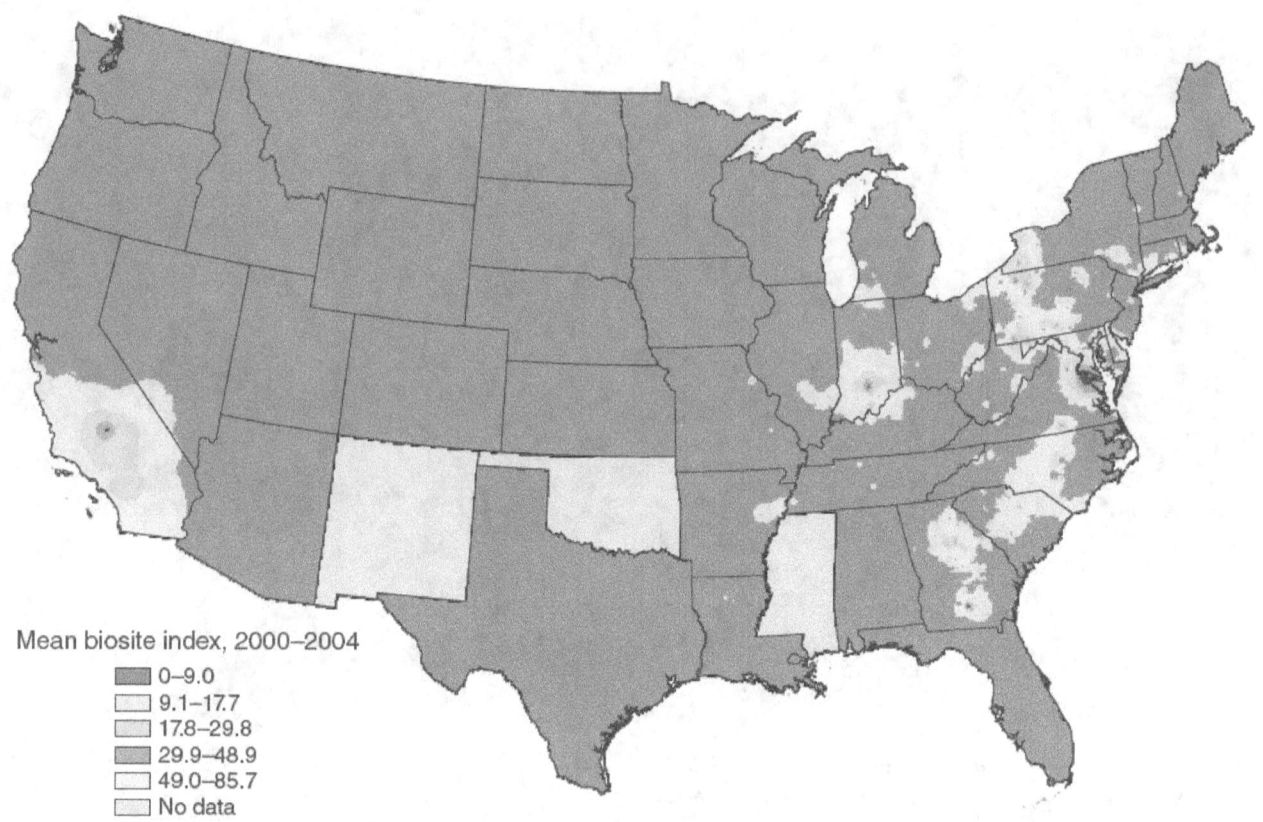

Mean biosite index, 2000–2004

- 0–9.0
- 9.1–17.7
- 17.8–29.8
- 29.9–48.9
- 49.0–85.7
- No data

Figure 54—Predicted ozone risk in the United States using inverse distance weighted interpolations of U.S. Forest Service measured ozone biosite index means, 2000–2004.

Birds foot violet (*Viola pedata* var. *lineariloba*).

Indicators of Forest Health

With the development of the Healthy Forest Initiative (see the President's Healthy Forest Initiative available online: http://www. whitehouse.gov/infocus/healthyforests/ Healthy_Forests_v2.pdf) and the Forest Service Chief's identification of Four Threats (fire and fuels, invasive species, loss of open space, and unmanaged recreation) to American Forests in the 21st Century (see http://www.fs.fed.us/projects/four-threats/), forest health has become a topic of great interest to the scientific and lay community. The Forest Service monitors forest health by measuring a combination of indicators, much as a doctor would monitor a patient's health by measuring indicators such as temperature, blood pressure, and weight (McCune 2000). Forest health indicators measured by the Forest Service FIA Program include crown structure, down woody material (DWM), soil characteristics, vegetation structure and diversity, lichen communities, and ozone damage. Through analysis of each of these variables at Statewide, regional, and national levels, scientists are able to identify potential problems and pinpoint areas of concern for intensified research programs. Additionally, trends may be detected and changes tracked over time. The forest health variables presented here for Tennessee reflect monitoring conducted by two programs that were merged in 2000: Forest Health Monitoring (FHM) and FIA. In Tennessee, Forest Health data collection includes variables related to crown structure, DWM, soil chemistry, and ozone damage.

Information about forest health is obtained in a variety of ways. First, FIA provides information in each State on rates of tree growth and death, harvesting, and changes in forest types and tree species. FIA and State agencies conduct regular ground and aerial surveys of forest damage and the causal agents, both in permanent plots and in other forest areas. In addition, universities, private industry, environmental groups, and other Forest Service scientists cooperate with FIA on a variety of forest research projects.

The FHM Program is a joint Federal/ State program aimed at understanding forest health. This national program was developed in 1990 and is under the administration of the Forest Service and partners with State foresters, other Federal and State agencies, and universities. The program goal is to monitor, assess, and report on the status, changes, and long-term trends in the health of our Nation's forests. The program involves a network of permanent plots and other off-plot areas that are regularly visited to monitor tree vigor, crown condition, and signs of damage. On a subset of the plots, plants are monitored for damage caused by ozone. Structure of the plant communities and presence of lichens (pollution-sensitive life forms that are a combination of algae and fungi) also are evaluated on a subset of the plots. The forest health information presented in this report comes primarily from FIA and FHM monitoring.

Mayapple (*Podophyllum pelatuem*) is a common sight in healthy forests.

What is a Healthy Forest?

From the spruce–fir forests of the Great Smoky Mountains National Park in east Tennessee to the bottomland hardwood forests within the Mississippi River floodplain of west Tennessee, Tennessee's forests are complex ecosystems, and they are vital to the State's overall well-being. Wildlife depend on them for habitat, and we humans depend on them for food, fiber, recreation, water quality, economic stability, and a variety of factors that affect our health.

Regardless of how people view the forests of Tennessee, the health of these forests is vital. But what is a healthy forest and how is it defined? Healthy compared to what and by what criteria? There are many definitions and concepts because how one views forest health is a reflection of personal values. While it may be difficult to explicitly define a "healthy forest," we can look at a number of indicators and synthesize the information into a larger picture of the health of the forests in the State. No single measurement or variable can summarize forest health. Instead, we must look at a wide set of indicators which together serve as a reflection of existing conditions. Repeated monitoring of the forest over time allows us to identify trends in forest conditions and evaluate the effectiveness of our actions.

For example, increased tree mortality can indicate a pest or disease issue, high levels of observed ozone damage may mean a problem with ozone pollution, or increasing observations of nonnative invasive species may warn of future ecological or economic problems. Numerous forest health indicators must be viewed holistically in order to gain an appreciation for the overall health of our forests and the numerous threats they may be facing. We can use this information to help improve the condition of the State's forests over time.

A multitude of different kinds of trees, herbaceous plants, animals, and microorganisms, as well as natural processes such as disturbances like fire, help maintain a healthy forest ecosystem. Careful management and harvesting also play a vital role in sustaining the health of forested ecosystems. Some things that have a negative impact on forest health are pests, diseases, and exotic invasive species, such as the hemlock wooly adelgid and the gypsy moth. In the past, large scale overharvesting had a major impact on forest health, especially when our country was young and relied heavily on forest resources. Large scale overharvesting was not an issue in Tennessee in 2004, but some forests were declining naturally as a result of increased age.

Hemlock wooly adelgid (*Adelges tsugae*) is a pest that has the potential to significantly alter forest systems in east Tennessee.

Deadwood in Tennessee Forest Land—Fuels and Habitat

Deadwood is extremely important to forest ecosystems because it performs a number of key ecological functions. For example, it serves as nurse logs for the growth of plants and moss, is critical to nutrient cycling and as an element of wildlife habitat, and is a major component of forest fuel loads (Waddell 2002, Bate and others 2004). A multitude of organisms rely on DWM to provide structural and/or thermal protection, foraging sites, or travel corridors (Bate and others 2004). For example, Mannan and others (1996) describe 13 small mammal species that depend on coarse woody material for all three of their life-history requirements: food, shelter, and reproduction. However, too much deadwood in the forest can result in excess fuel loads, sustaining damaging wildfires over large areas. Therefore, forest managers must strike a balance between maintaining enough deadwood to sustain wildlife, insect, and plant communities and avoiding unacceptably high fuel accumulations.

Despite the importance of deadwood to a variety of organisms and ecosystem functions, little attention has been given to the distribution of woody material on the landscape until relatively recently (Waddell 2002). FIA quantifies the amount and extent of fine and coarse woody debris on the forested landscape, and the number of snags present in the forest.

Deadwood as habitat—Snags, hollow logs, and brush piles provide important habitat for vertebrate communities, while decaying plant material, litter, and duff provide important habitat for micro- and macroinvertebrates. Many types of vegetation rely on decaying plant material as a growth substrate. Deadwood is not distributed evenly across the landscape, nor is it equally important for wildlife in every forest. For example, live deciduous trees in eastern forests often contain cavities that provide habitat for cavity-nesting animals, decreasing the number of standing dead trees necessary to provide quality nest sites (Mannan and others 1996). In contrast, cavity-nesting animals living in the coniferous forests of the Southeastern United States and the Western United States may be more dependent on standing dead trees as appropriate habitat, increasing the number necessary to provide optimum habitat (Mannan and others 1996). The size and stage of decay of a snag also influence the type and number of animals that can use the tree. Generally, trees larger than 14-inches diameter at breast height (d.b.h.) are preferred for nesting, though snags of any size or decay class can provide food resources for multiple animals (Mannan and others 1996). The optimal number of snags to retain for wildlife on each acre of forest land depends on multiple conditions, including the management goals for the forest, the wildlife species present or desired, and the size, age, and species of trees present.

FIA collects data on snags on all Phase 2 sample plots Statewide. In 2004, there were about 168 million standing dead trees over 5-inches d.b.h. on Tennessee forest land. Statewide, hardwoods provided the largest number of snags on Tennessee's forests in 2004 (fig. 55). However, softwood snags outnumbered hardwood snags on the Plateau and in the East—areas heavily impacted by the SPB (fig. 56). Small snags

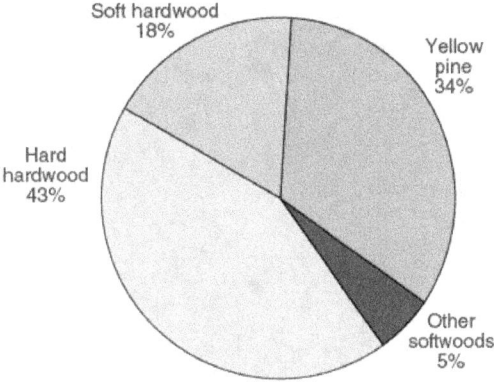

Figure 55—Standing-dead trees by major species group for Tennessee, 2004.

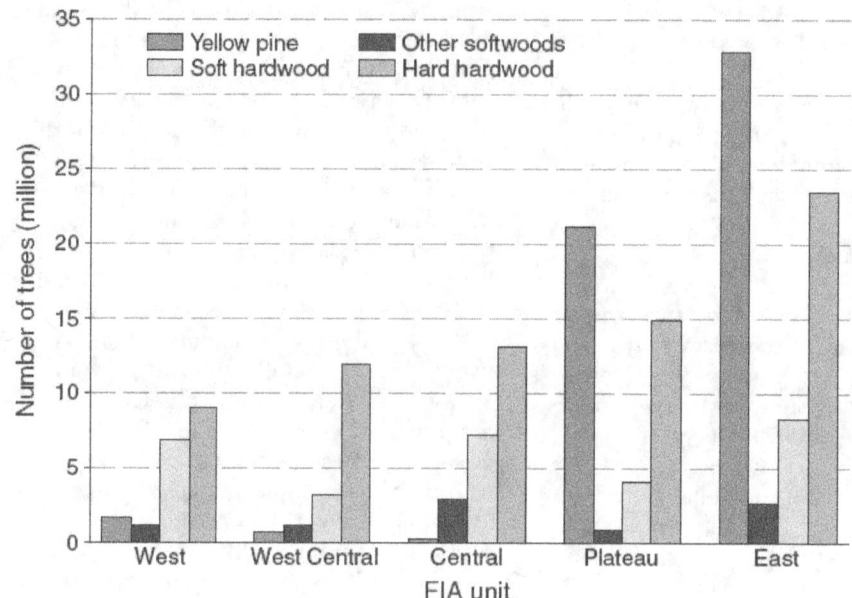

Figure 56—Number of standing-dead trees > 5 inches in diameter by major species group and FIA unit in Tennessee, 2004.

(5.0- to 13.9-inches d.b.h.) outnumbered large snags (> 14 inches d.b.h.) by 9 to 1. There were an average of 12 snags per acre of forest land in Tennessee. The number of snags per acre varies across the State, with the lowest per acre concentrations in the West Central units, and the highest per acre concentrations in the East and Plateau units.

Hollow logs and other types of coarse woody material also provide shelter or food for many species during at least some portion of their life-history cycle. Information on coarse woody material was collected on 128 Forest Health plots

across the State of Tennessee from 2001 to 2004. Measurements of the size and decay class of individual pieces of wood provide information about the suitability of logs for use by wildlife, and the recruitment of new dead material onto the forest floor. Most of the coarse material sampled in 2001–2004 was moderately to heavily decayed (decay classes 3 and 4) (fig. 57), and fell into the

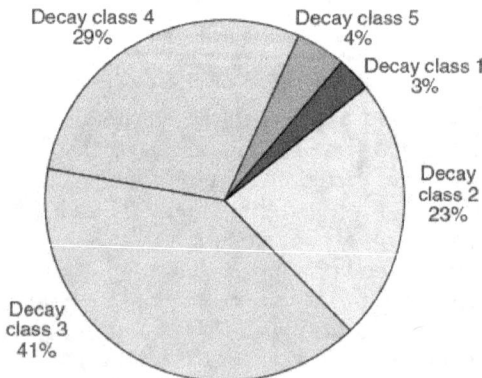

Figure 57—Proportion of coarse woody material by decay class, Tennessee, 2001–2004.

smallest diameter class (3.0- to 7.9-inches d.b.h.). The largest quantities of coarse woody material (1,000-hour fuels) occurred in the loblolly-shortleaf pine, oak-hickory, and oak-pine forest-type groups (table 10), and more down deadwood (fine and coarse material combined, excluding slash material) occurred on the Plateau and in the East than in any other region (table 11).

Table 10—State-level means of down woody materials by forest-type group and fuel type, Tennessee, 2004

Forest-type group (n)	1-hour	10-hour	100-hour	1,000-hour	Duff	Litter	Slash piles	Total tons all fuels	Total tons excluding slash
				tons per acre					
White-red-jack (3)	0.22	0.43	1.49	1.60	8.71	1.78	0.00	14.51	14.51
Loblolly-shortleaf (14)	0.27	1.39	1.31	2.75	12.41	5.07	0.61	23.89	23.28
Pinyon-juniper (E. redcedar) (7)	0.22	0.45	1.36	0.59	6.52	1.52	0.00	10.86	10.86
Oak-pine (14)	0.19	0.77	1.75	2.02	10.29	5.73	1.43	22.36	20.92
Oak-hickory (108)	0.24	0.84	2.12	2.84	9.11	3.05	15.80	33.92	18.12
Oak-gum-cypress (5)	0.30	1.12	3.97	1.35	6.96	1.86	0.00	15.57	15.57
Elm-ash-cottonwood (6)	0.17	0.68	0.85	0.54	2.77	1.12	0.00	6.25	6.25
Maple-beech-birch (1)	0.50	0.61	2.72	0.51	1.81	0.32	0.00	7.18	7.18

n = sample size; all estimates are tons per acre unless otherwise indicated.

[a] 1-hour = small fine woody; 10-hour = medium fine woody; 100-hour = large fine woody; 1,000 hour = coarse fine woody (see glossary).

Table 11—State-level means of down woody materials by FIA unit and fuel type, Tennessee, 2004

FIA unit (n)	1-hour	10-hour	100-hour	1,000-hour	Duff	Litter	Slash piles	Total tons all fuels	Total tons excluding slash
				tons per acre					
West (23)	0.25	0.66	1.81	2.15	5.64	3.22	0.00	13.70	13.70
West Central (22)	0.29	1.06	1.93	2.43	6.37	2.66	1.29	16.05	14.76
Central (26)	0.21	0.62	1.33	1.85	6.36	2.12	0.00	12.82	12.82
Plateau (35)	0.21	0.91	2.43	3.31	10.20	4.20	20.93	41.89	20.96
East (52)	0.23	0.86	2.16	2.40	11.87	3.24	20.00	40.81	20.81

n = sample size; all estimates are tons per acre unless otherwise indicated.

[a] 1-hour = small fine woody; 10-hour = medium fine woody; 100-hour = large fine woody; 1,000 hour = coarse fine woody (see glossary).

It can be exciting to run across a copperhead snake (*Agkistrodon contortix*) while enjoying one of Tennessee's numerous forests.

A Table Mountain pine forest (*Pinus pungens*) following a prescribed fire designed to help regenerate a scarce species in Tennessee.

Deadwood as fuel—As a natural event and a silvicultural tool, fire influences every aspect of forest ecology, including soil chemistry, wildlife habitat, biomass storage, and plant composition (Barnes and others 1998). Some tree species are dependent on forest fires to complete portions of their life cycles. For example, some conifers have evolved serotinous (closed) cones that require heat from fire to open. Other species have developed thick leaves and bark that resist fire damage, or seeds that

require heat for germination (Barnes and others 1998). Many wildlife species also favor conditions established by forest fires. The stimulation of plant growth resulting from forest fires benefits small and large game in southern forests. Fires also promote the development of live-tree cavities suitable for black bears (Mannan and others 1996).

Forest fires are not always beneficial, however. Federal spending on wildfire suppression and prevention can reach $500 million per year (Butry and others 2001). Beyond economic losses, catastrophic fires increase air pollution through the emission of carbon monoxide, hydrocarbons, and volatile organic compounds (McMahon 1983). Additionally, intense wildfires can increase the rate of erosion on steep sites as soils are exposed (Barnes and others 1998).

In order to catch and burn, a fire requires three primary ingredients: an ignition source, oxygen, and fuel. Surface fuels include the duff (partially decomposed organic matter) and litter (leaves, twigs, and other small pieces of organic matter) layers of the forest floor, fine woody debris and slash piles, and finally, coarse woody debris (McMahon 1983). The accumulation of large amounts of surface fuels, particularly fine woody debris and slash, increases the potential risk of catastrophic wildfire given the appropriate weather conditions and an ignition source. Small (1-hour and 10-hour) fuels tend to dry out rapidly and ignite quickly, while large (100-hour and 1,000-hour) fuels tend to retain moisture and smolder rather than ignite (Schulz 2003). Tennessee averaged 0.2 tons per acre of 1-hour, 1.0 tons per acre of 10-hour, 3.2 tons per acre of 100-hour fine woody fuels, and 2.5 tons per acre of 1,000-hour coarse fuels on forest land from 2001 to 2004 (figs. 58 and 59).

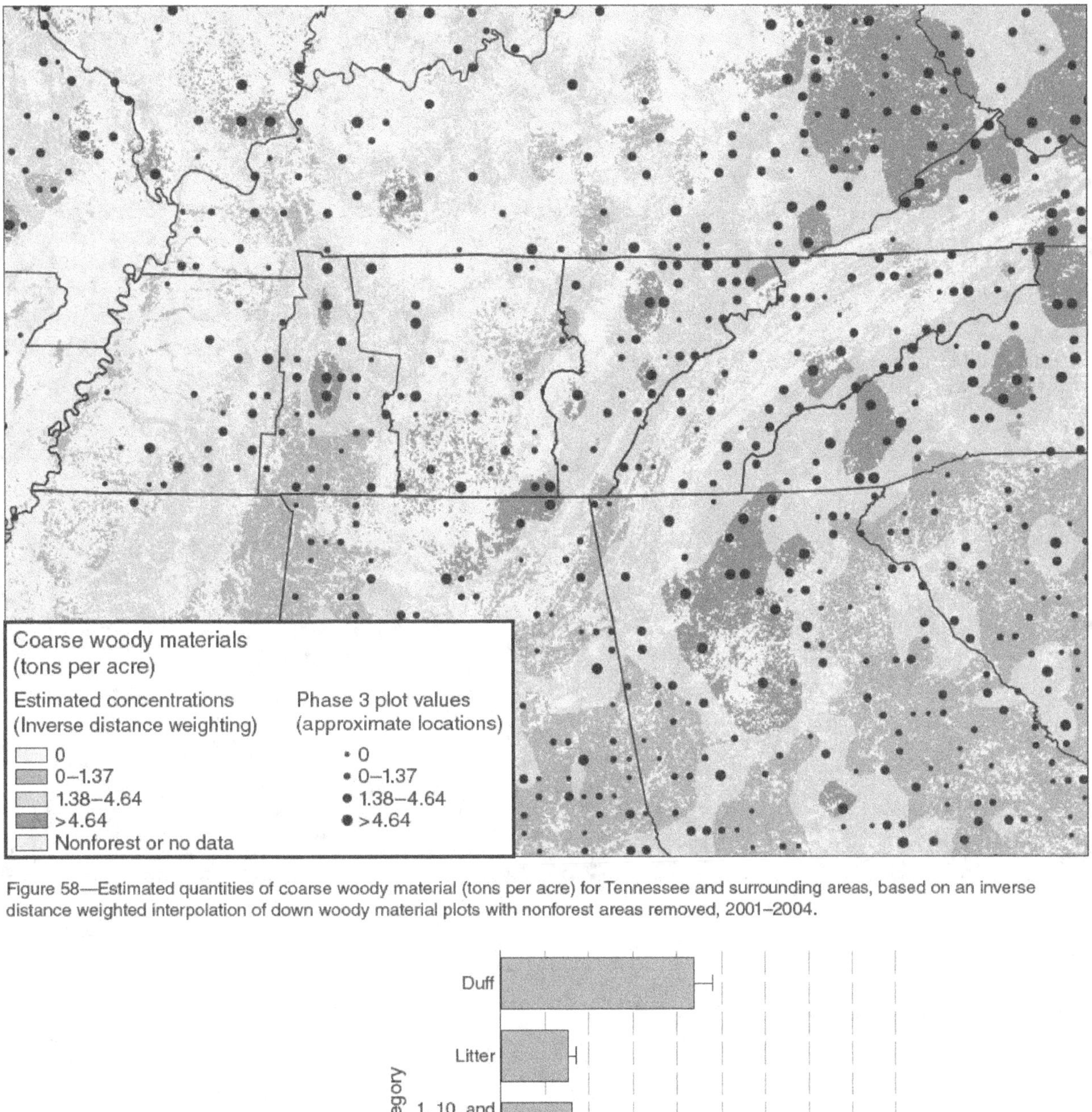

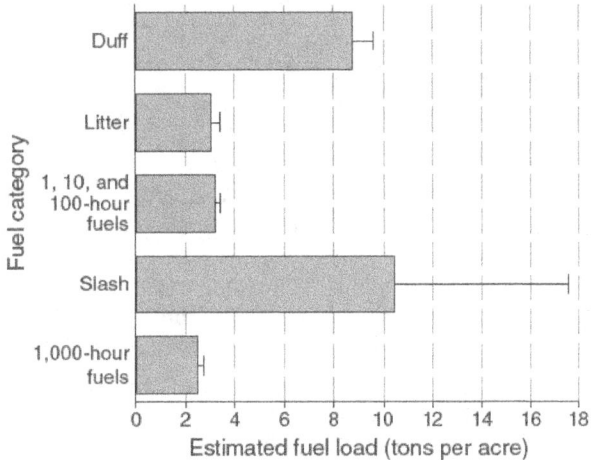

Figure 58—Estimated quantities of coarse woody material (tons per acre) for Tennessee and surrounding areas, based on an inverse distance weighted interpolation of down woody material plots with nonforest areas removed, 2001–2004.

Figure 59—Estimated fuel loads in Tennessee by fuel category, 2001–2004.

Flowering dogwood
(*Cornus florida*) are
common in forests
of Tennessee.

Tree Crown Health

FIA includes visual assessments of
individual tree crown condition on the
Phase 3 (see "Glossary") subset of its
inventory plots to aid the monitoring
of changes and trends in forest health
(Schomaker and others 2007). Tree crown
condition can be used to track forest health
because a tree undergoing stress reacts
by slowing growth and shedding parts of
its crown (Millers and others 1989). The
shedding of foliage and fine twigs not only
changes the tree's appearance but also alters
its rate of photosynthesis and carbohydrate
production. Thus, poor crown conditions
can be a signal of declining growth rates and
degraded forest health. Unfortunately, we

do not know exactly what crown condition
values indicate the point at which trees
begin to decline biologically. Thresholds
based on statistical distributions have
been used in the past (e.g., Bechtold and
others 1992); however, these thresholds
are subjective and have been applied
without regard to species and normal stand
dynamics. Establishment of biological
thresholds is ongoing, but will require
repeated measurements of the Phase 3 plots.
Presently, point-in-time estimates of crown
condition are reported and examined for
anomalies that might suggest an underlying
forest health problem.

The following crown conditions were
recorded on the Phase 3 plots in Tennessee
for trees ≥ 5.0-inches d.b.h. This summary

includes 4 years of assessment, 2000–2002 and 2004. Data from 2003 were not available at the time of writing. Each of the three crown condition variables was visually assessed by a two-person field crew and recorded in 5-percent increments from 0 to 99 percent. Overall, average crown conditions in Tennessee were within the expected range for trees in the Southern United States and seem representative of values for healthy and productive trees.

Crown density—Crown density is the percentage of light blocked through the projected crown outline by live and dead branches, foliage, and reproductive structures. Crown density is a measure of the amount of foliage present on the tree, and greater crown densities are typically associated with healthy trees. Average crown density was 36.8 percent for softwoods and 41.0 percent for hardwoods (table 12). These averages are typical for trees in the Southern United States. In the absence of decline, average crown densities typically vary in a consistent manner by species because shade tolerance and leaf and branch morphology affect crown condition. Among the hardwoods, American beech typically maintains some

Table 12—Mean crown density and other statistics[a] for all live trees ≥ 5.0-inches d.b.h., by species, Tennessee inventory panels 1–4 (2000–2002, 2004)

Species	Plots	Trees	Mean	SE[b]	Minimum	Median	Maximum
	--- number ---		---------------- percent ----------------				
Softwoods							
Eastern redcedar	18	80	39.8	1.5	5	40	70
Shortleaf pine	11	32	38.4	2.3	30	35	60
Pitch pine	3	12	37.5	—	20	40	45
Loblolly pine	11	208	34.6	1.3	15	35	55
Virginia pine	17	98	37.3	1.0	5	35	60
Other softwoods	9	27	40.2	1.1	25	40	55
Total	49	457	36.8	1.1	5	35	70
Hardwoods							
White oaks	77	424	40.4	0.6	0	40	70
Red oaks	66	216	39.1	0.5	5	40	60
Maple	73	312	40.6	0.9	0	40	65
Sweetgum	29	110	42.0	1.5	10	40	70
Yellow-poplar	60	220	42.9	1.1	0	45	70
Blackgum	34	62	41.9	1.5	5	40	70
Hickory	61	238	43.6	0.8	10	45	65
Ash	35	93	40.9	1.7	5	40	70
Elm	31	73	38.4	1.0	10	40	60
Persimmon	11	20	40.5	3.1	15	40	55
American beech	16	32	44.5	1.9	30	45	60
Sourwood	35	78	39.8	1.1	10	40	60
Black cherry	28	52	39.3	1.8	0	40	75
Sassafras	13	24	37.7	3.2	20	37.5	55
Other hardwoods	60	173	40.3	0.9	20	40	65
Total	119	2,127	41.0	0.4	0	40	75
Species total	121	2,584	40.2	0.5	0	40	75

SE = standard error; — = not presented due to insufficient sample.

[a] The mean and standard error calculations consider the clustering of trees on plots.

[b] Standard errors are not presented for species groups with n trees < 20.

Eastern hemlock (*Tsuga canadensis*).

of the densest crowns, and species such as black locust and flowering dogwood maintain less dense crowns. Among the softwoods, eastern hemlock and eastern redcedar tend to have the densest crowns while Virginia pine has very sparse crowns. Crown density in Tennessee generally followed the expected pattern (table 12). Average crown density was highest for eastern redcedar and lowest for loblolly pine and Virginia pine among the softwoods. Among the hardwoods, average crown density was highest for American beech and lowest for sassafras (table 12).

Crown dieback—Crown dieback is a measure of recent stress identified by the mortality of fine twigs and branches in the upper and outer portion of the crown. Crown dieback is typically a symptom of severe stress, though normal physiological processes may also induce some dieback (e.g., excessive seed production) (Millers and others 1992). Light dieback typically occurs more often in hardwoods than in conifers. Overall, 88.1 percent of trees in Tennessee had no crown dieback. Average dieback was 1.4 percent for softwoods and 1.9 percent for hardwoods (table 13).

Table 13—Mean crown dieback and other statistics[a] for all live trees ≥ 5.0-inches d.b.h., by species, Tennessee inventory panels 1–4 (2000–2002, 2004)

Species	Plots	Trees	Mean	SE[b]	Minimum	90th percentile	Maximum
	- - - number - - -		- - - - - - - - - - - - - - - - - percent - - - - - - - - - - - - - - - - -				
Softwoods							
Eastern redcedar	18	80	2.7	1.7	0	5	80
Shortleaf pine	11	32	0.8	0.4	0	5	5
Pitch pine	3	12	1.7	—	0	5	15
Loblolly pine	11	208	0.7	0.5	0	5	10
Virginia pine	17	98	2.1	1.4	0	5	90
Other softwoods	9	27	0.6	0.4	0	0	10
Total	49	457	1.4	0.5	0	5	90
Hardwoods							
White oaks	77	424	1.4	0.3	0	5	99
Red oaks	66	216	3.0	0.6	0	10	75
Maple	73	312	1.8	0.6	0	0	99
Sweetgum	29	110	1.9	0.9	0	5	60
Yellow-poplar	60	220	1.5	0.6	0	0	99
Blackgum	34	62	1.9	1.3	0	0	85
Hickory	61	238	1.6	0.7	0	0	85
Ash	35	93	2.7	1.5	0	5	90
Elm	31	73	1.7	0.5	0	5	30
Common persimmon	11	20	1.3	0.7	0	8	10
American beech	16	32	0.2	0.1	0	0	5
Sourwood	35	78	3.5	1.6	0	5	70
Black cherry	28	52	3.3	2.0	0	5	99
Sassafras	13	24	1.5	0.8	0	5	15
Other hardwoods	60	173	1.4	0.4	0	5	40
Total	119	2,127	1.9	0.3	0	5	99
Species total	121	2,584	1.8	0.2	0	5	99

SE = standard error; — = not presented due to insufficient sample.

[a] The mean and standard error calculations consider the clustering of trees on plots.

[b] Standard errors are not presented for species groups with *n* trees < 20.

Foliage transparency—Foliage transparency is measured as the amount of skylight visible through the live, normally foliated portion of the crown. Foliage transparency is an indicator of the amount of foliage present on the tree and thus is related to growth potential. Typically, lower foliage transparency ratings indicate healthy trees. As with crown density, average foliage transparency tends to be species specific; however, there is less variation among the foliage transparency averages than there is among the crown density averages. Average foliage transparency in Tennessee was 22.0 percent for all softwoods and ranged from a low of 19.6 percent for loblolly pine to a high of 26.1 percent for Virginia pine (table 14). Foliage transparency averaged 20.1 percent for all hardwoods and ranged from a low of 18.4 percent for yellow-poplar to a high of 23.5 percent for black cherry.

Table 14—Mean foliage transparency and other statistics[a] for all live trees ≥ 5.0-inches d.b.h., by species, Tennessee inventory panels 1–4 (2000–2002, 2004)

Species	Plots	Trees	Mean	SE[b]	Minimum	Median	Maximum
	- - - number - - -		- - - - - - - - - - - - - - - - percent - - - - - - - - - - - - - - - -				
Softwoods							
Eastern redcedar	18	80	21.4	1.3	10	20	35
Shortleaf pine	11	32	25.0	1.8	15	25	40
Pitch pine	3	12	23.3	—	20	20	35
Loblolly pine	11	208	19.6	1.9	5	20	35
Virginia pine	17	98	26.1	1.2	0	25	80
Other softwoods	9	27	23.0	0.9	15	20	30
Total	49	457	22.0	1.3	0	20	80
Hardwoods							
White oaks	77	424	20.4	0.4	5	20	99
Red oaks	66	216	20.8	0.5	10	20	70
Maple	73	312	20.3	0.7	0	20	99
Sweetgum	29	110	20.1	0.6	10	20	35
Yellow poplar	60	220	18.4	0.9	5	20	99
Blackgum	34	62	19.0	0.9	5	20	40
Hickory	61	238	18.8	0.8	10	20	30
Ash	35	93	21.5	0.8	5	20	30
Elm	31	73	21.2	0.9	10	20	45
Common persimmon	11	20	20.3	1.0	10	20	30
American beech	16	32	19.2	1.5	5	20	30
Sourwood	35	78	19.6	0.6	5	20	30
Black cherry	28	52	23.5	1.7	0	25	99
Sassafras	13	24	19.2	1.1	15	20	30
Other hardwoods	60	173	21.1	0.9	10	20	70
Total	119	2,127	20.1	0.4	0	20	99
Species total	121	2,584	20.5	0.4	0	20	99

SE = standard error; — = not presented due to insufficient sample.

[a] The mean and standard error calculations consider the clustering of trees on plots.

[b] Standard errors are not presented for species groups with n trees < 20.

Socioeconomic Benefits of Tennessee Forests

Through the practice of silviculture, foresters attempt to control or influence the development of forests for healthy, sustainable forest communities while supplying humankind with a myriad of values. The goal of silvicultural prescriptions is to guide and direct change within forested systems toward a desired end.

Timber Products and the Economy

Tennessee's forest products industry is an important component of the State's economy. According to IMPLAN (IMpact Analysis for PLANning) (U.S. Department of Agriculture 2004b), a model generated by the Forest Service, the total economic importance of Tennessee's forests in 2001 was more than $16.1 billion. This figure includes all activities associated with the forest products industry which includes direct, indirect, and induced effects resulting from the industry operation.

In 2004, about 450 sawmills, pulpwood mills, and other primary wood-processing plants distributed across the State

(fig. 60) directly employed more than 31,700 individuals, with an annual payroll of $1.0 billion. In 2004, the total value of shipments in Tennessee's wood products and paper manufacturing sectors exceeded $6.9 billion (U.S. Department of Commerce 2005). Figures in table 15 show employment, payroll, and value of shipments for Tennessee for the years 1999–2004. While the number of employees declined nearly 18 percent between 1999 and 2004, payroll declined 4 percent, or more than $48 million, between 1999 and 2004. At the same time, value of shipments increased 5 percent from $6.8 billion in 1999 to $7.2 billion in 2004.

Timber Products Output and Removals

This section presents estimates of average annual roundwood product output and timber removals for the period 1999–2004. Estimates of timber product output (TPO) and plant residues were obtained from canvasses (questionnaires) sent to all primary wood-using mills in the State. The canvasses are used to determine the types and amount of roundwood (i.e., saw logs, pulpwood, poles, etc.) received by each

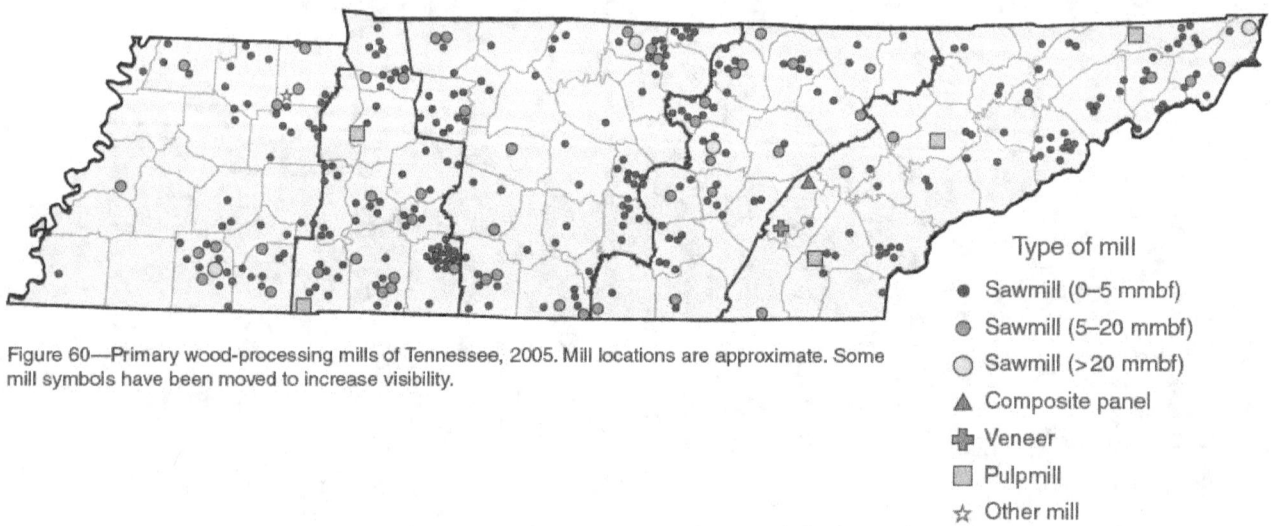

Figure 60—Primary wood-processing mills of Tennessee, 2005. Mill locations are approximate. Some mill symbols have been moved to increase visibility.

Type of mill
- Sawmill (0–5 mmbf)
- Sawmill (5–20 mmbf)
- Sawmill (>20 mmbf)
- ▲ Composite panel
- Veneer
- ■ Pulpmill
- ☆ Other mill

mill, the county of origin of the wood, the species used, and how the mills dispose of the bark and wood residues produced. The canvasses are conducted every 2 years by personnel from the Tennessee Department of Agriculture, Division of Forestry, and the Southern Research Station. These data are used to augment FIA's annual inventory of timber removals by providing the product proportions for that segment of removals that is used for products. Individual studies are necessary to track trends and changes in product output levels. Industry surveys conducted in 1999, 2001, and 2003 were used to determine average annual product output for roundwood and plant byproducts. Total product output, averaged over the survey period, is the sum of the volume of roundwood products from all sources (growing stock and other sources) and the volume of plant byproducts, or the mill residues.

Total output of timber products, which includes domestic fuelwood and plant byproducts, averaged nearly 437 million cubic feet per year between 1999 and 2004, a 1-percent increase from the previous period between 1989 and 1998 (table 16). Eighty-six percent, or 375 million cubic feet, of the total output was from roundwood products, while the remainder was from plant byproducts (mill residue). Hardwood species provided 302 million cubic feet, or 69 percent, of the total product output volume. Softwoods provided the remaining 31 percent, or 135 million cubic feet of total output.

Table 15—U.S. Census Bureau statistics for the wood product and paper manufacturing industry groups, Tennessee, 1999 to 2004

Year	Employees	Payroll	Shipments
	number	- - - thousand dollars - - -	
1999	37,314	1,124,588	6,848,617
2000	37,208	1,169,736	7,271,796
2001	34,794	1,108,256	6,808,651
2002	32,380	1,068,387	6,688,293
2003	31,779	1,049,181	6,902,884
2004	30,500	1,076,166	7,216,354
Average	33,996	1,099,386	6,956,099

Recently harvested pine logs ready to be delivered to the mill.

Table 16—Average annual output of timber products by product, species group, and type of material, Tennessee, 1999 to 2004

Product and species group	Total output	Roundwood products	Plant byproducts
		million cubic feet	
Saw logs			
Softwood	31.6	31.6	—
Hardwood	151.3	151.3	—
Total	182.9	182.9	—
Veneer logs			
Softwood	3.6	3.6	—
Hardwood	1.4	1.4	—
Total	5.1	5.1	—
Pulpwood			
Softwood	58.1	55.1	3.0
Hardwood	104.7	72.0	32.7
Total	162.9	127.2	35.7
Poles and pilings			
Softwood	0.4	0.4	—
Hardwood	—	—	—
Total	0.4	0.4	—
Posts			
Softwood	1.1	1.1	—
Hardwood	—	—	—
Total	1.1	1.1	—
Other industrial[a]			
Softwood	22.0	17.5	4.5
Hardwood	21.1	1.1	20.0
Total	43.1	18.6	24.5
Total industrial products			
Softwood	116.9	109.4	7.5
Hardwood	278.7	225.9	52.7
Total	395.5	335.3	60.3
Fuelwood[b]			
Softwood	18.5	18.5	—
Hardwood	22.9	21.6	1.3
Total	41.3	40.1	1.3
All products			
Softwood	135.4	127.8	7.5
Hardwood	301.5	247.5	54.0
Total	436.9	375.4	61.5

Numbers in rows and columns may not sum to totals due to rounding.

— = no sample for the cell.

[a] Includes litter, mulch, particleboard, charcoal, and other specialty products.

[b] Excludes approximately 32.4 million cubic feet of wood residues and 18.8 million cubic feet of bark used for industrial fuel.

Saw logs were the primary wood product produced by Tennessee's mills between 1999 and 2004, accounting for 42 percent of the total TPO volume during that period. Production of saw logs used mainly for dimension lumber increased 5 percent from 174 million cubic feet in 1998 to 183 million cubic feet in 2004. Between 1999 and 2004, hardwood saw-log production declined 3 percent to 151 million cubic feet, while softwood saw-log production increased 78 percent to 32 million cubic feet. However, hardwoods still accounted for nearly 83 percent of the total saw-log output during the latest survey period. The production of pulpwood followed closely behind saw-log production, increasing from 139 million cubic feet in 1998 to 163 million cubic feet during the latest survey period. Between 1999 and 2004 pulpwood output was up nearly 18 percent, and accounted for 37 percent of the total output volume. Hardwood pulpwood production totaled 105 million cubic feet and accounted for 64 percent of total pulpwood production, while softwood pulpwood production amounted to 58 million cubic feet. Plant byproducts, or mill residue, accounted for 31 and 5 percent, respectively, of total hardwood and softwood pulpwood production. The 36 million cubic feet of plant byproducts used for pulpwood production accounted for 59 percent of mill residue utilized for industrial products (table 17). Other industrial products, which includes poles, posts, and composite panel products totaled nearly 46 million cubic feet and accounted for 10 percent of total product output. Veneer production amounted to 5 million cubic feet and accounted for only 1 percent of total output. Domestic fuelwood totaled 41 million cubic feet, and accounted for

Table 17—Average annual output of roundwood products by product, primary wood-using plants by product, species group, and type of residue, Tennessee, 1999 to 2004

Product and species group	All types	Bark	Coarse[a]	Fine
		million cubic feet		
Fiber products				
Softwood	3.0	—	2.9	0.1
Hardwood	32.7	—	31.8	0.9
Total	35.7	—	34.8	0.9
Particleboard				
Softwood	0.3	—	0.3	0.0
Hardwood	3.0	0.0	2.7	0.3
Total	3.2	0.0	3.0	0.3
Sawn products				
Softwood	—	—	—	—
Hardwood	—	—	—	—
Total	—	—	—	—
Industrial fuel				
Softwood	12.9	9.9	0.9	2.1
Hardwood	38.2	8.9	6.7	22.6
Total	51.1	18.8	7.6	24.8
Domestic fuel				
Softwood	—	—	—	—
Hardwood	1.3	—	1.3	—
Total	1.3	—	1.3	—
Miscellaneous				
Softwood	4.2	2.9	0.4	0.9
Hardwood	17.1	9.1	3.7	4.2
Total	21.3	12.0	4.2	5.2
Not used				
Softwood	1.2	0.1	0.7	0.4
Hardwood	10.7	2.1	5.7	3.0
Total	11.9	2.2	6.4	3.3
All products				
Softwood	21.7	12.9	5.2	3.5
Hardwood	103.0	20.1	51.9	30.9
Total	124.6	33.0	57.2	34.5

Numbers in rows and columns may not sum to totals due to rounding.

— = no sample for the cell; 0.0 = a value of > 0.0 but < 0.05 for the cell.

[a] Material such as slabs and edgings.

nearly 10 percent of total product output for the State. Plant byproducts used for industrial fuel amounted to 51 million cubic feet accounting for 45 percent of the utilized mill byproducts.

Figure 61 shows trends in average annual roundwood product output from 1961 through 2004. While roundwood used for most industrial products was up, roundwood used for domestic fuelwood was down significantly from the previous survey period. Average annual output of roundwood products (including fuelwood) declined nearly 3 percent, or 10 million cubic feet, from 385 million cubic feet in the previous survey period, to an average of 375 million cubic feet between 1999 and 2004. Softwood roundwood production increased

nearly 54 percent to 128 million cubic feet, while hardwood roundwood production declined 18 percent to 248 million cubic feet. Annual roundwood saw log and pulpwood production amounted to 183 and 127 million cubic feet, respectively. These two products accounted for 83 percent of the total roundwood production for the State between 1999 and 2004. Ninety-three percent of the roundwood products volume came from growing-stock trees, split between sawtimber (80 percent) and poletimber (20 percent) trees (table 18). Other sources, which include cull trees, salvable dead trees, and stumps and tops of harvested trees, dropped from 70 million cubic feet reported in the previous survey period to 26 million cubic feet.

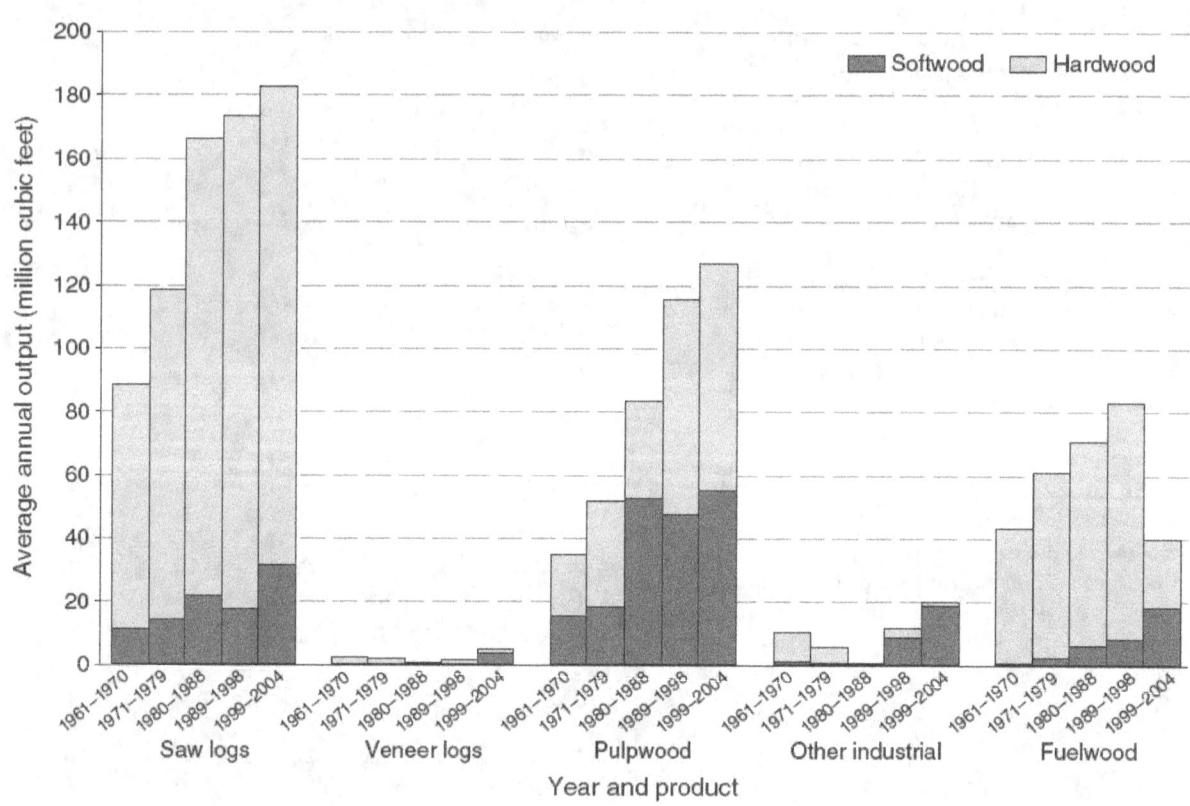

Figure 61—Average annual output of roundwood timber products by product and species group, Tennessee, 1961 through 2004.

Table 18—Average annual output of timber products by product, species group, and source of material, Tennessee, 1999 to 2004

Product and species group	All sources	Growing-stock trees[a]			Other sources
		Total	Sawtimber	Poletimber	
			million cubic feet		
Saw logs					
Softwood	31.6	30.8	29.1	1.7	0.8
Hardwood	151.3	147.8	138.9	8.9	3.5
Total	182.9	178.6	168.1	10.5	4.3
Veneer logs					
Softwood	3.6	3.5	3.5	—	0.1
Hardwood	1.4	1.4	1.4	—	0.0
Total	5.1	5.0	5.0	—	0.1
Pulpwood					
Softwood	55.1	50.0	31.2	18.8	5.1
Hardwood	72.0	64.5	36.8	27.7	7.5
Total	127.2	114.5	68.0	46.5	12.6
Poles and pilings					
Softwood	0.4	0.4	0.4	0.0	0.0
Hardwood	—	—	—	—	—
Total	0.4	0.4	0.4	0.0	0.0
Posts					
Softwood	1.1	1.1	0.6	0.5	0.1
Hardwood	—	—	—	—	—
Total	1.1	1.1	0.6	0.5	0.1
Other industrial					
Softwood	17.5	15.6	12.3	3.3	1.8
Hardwood	1.1	1.1	0.9	0.2	0.0
Total	18.6	16.7	13.3	3.5	1.9
Total industrial products					
Softwood	109.4	101.5	77.2	24.3	7.9
Hardwood	225.9	214.8	178.0	36.8	11.1
Total	335.3	316.3	255.3	61.0	19.0
Fuelwood					
Softwood	18.5	16.4	12.2	4.3	2.0
Hardwood	21.6	16.4	13.0	3.5	5.2
Total	40.1	32.8	25.1	7.7	7.2
All products					
Softwood	127.8	117.9	89.4	28.5	9.9
Hardwood	247.5	231.2	191.0	40.2	16.3
Total	375.4	349.1	280.4	68.8	26.2

Numbers in rows and columns may not sum to totals due to rounding.

— = no sample for the cell; 0.0 = a value of > 0.0 but < 0.05 for the cell.

[a] On timberland.

Total timber removals, averaged over the period 1999–2004, are the sum of the volume of roundwood products, logging residues (unused portions of trees left in the woods), and other removals (removals attributed to land clearing or land use changes) from growing-stock and nongrowing-stock sources. Annual removals from all sources, for both softwoods and hardwoods combined, averaged 783 million cubic feet (table 19) over the period 1999–2004. Hardwoods accounted for 71 percent of total removals. Volume used for roundwood products totaled 375 million cubic feet, or 48 percent, of total removals. Logging residues and other removals amounted to 241 million cubic feet (31 percent) and 166 million cubic feet (21 percent), respectively. These volumes were up significantly from those reported for 1989–1998. Logging residue was up due to the salvage efforts for the massive beetle kill early in the survey period, while other removals were affected by a reclassification of timberland plots to a reserved status mostly on other public lands.

Nontimber Forest Products

Tennessee has an active and vibrant industry based on nontimber forest products (NTFP). These products originate from fungi, moss, lichen, herbs, vines, shrubs, or trees. They are made from roots, tubers, leaves, bark, twigs, branches, fruit, and sap, as well as wood that is gathered but not cut from timber. The products are not included in the traditional definition of the forest products industry, but they have important uses in the herbal medicine, culinary, crafts, and floral and landscaping industries. They range from edible products (fruits, nuts, mushrooms, ramps, and maple syrup), to medicinal-type products (ginseng and bloodroot), to ornamental products (galax, pine tips for garlands, and grapevines), to landscape products (native plants), to specialty woods (burl and crotch wood for fine crafts).

A survey of county extension agents, with a response rate of almost 94 percent, which was designed to estimate the number and distribution of NTFP enterprises in Southern United States, indicated that Tennessee had a total of 2,572 NTFP firms as of April 2003 (Chamberlain and Predny 2003). The State ranked third behind Kentucky and North Carolina in total number of NTFP enterprises in the region, accounting for about 10 percent of the total (table 20).

Table 19—Average annual output of timber products by removals class, species group, and source, Tennessee, 1999 to 2004

Removals class and species group	All sources	Source Growing stock	Nongrowing stock
	million cubic feet		
Roundwood products			
Softwood	127.8	117.9	9.9
Hardwood	247.5	231.2	16.3
Total	375.4	349.1	26.2
Logging residues			
Softwood	84.0	23.4	60.6
Hardwood	157.4	45.6	111.8
Total	241.4	69.0	172.4
Other removals			
Softwood	17.3	15.7	1.6
Hardwood	149.1	125.3	23.9
Total	166.4	141.0	25.5
Total removals			
Softwood	229.1	157.0	72.1
Hardwood	554.0	402.1	151.9
Total	783.2	559.1	224.0

Numbers in rows and columns may not sum to totals due to rounding.

It ranked third in the South in number of firms that specialize in products made from medicinal plants, accounting for 314 (7 percent) of such enterprises. It ranked second in number of specialty wood products firms with 794 (19 percent) of such enterprises, and fourth in number of firms that specialize in edible forest products with 390 (10 percent) of such enterprises. Tennessee ranked fourth in firms that make floral and decorative products (481, or 7 percent) from wild-harvested materials and fourth in the region for firms (593, or 10 percent of total) that use native plants and plants collected from the wild for landscaping.

According to county extension agents, Tennessee had in 2003 a vast diversity of enterprises that used nontimber forests resources in the manufacture of products (fig. 62). About 12 percent of the estimated 2,572 NTFP enterprises in Tennessee dealt with medicinal plants. In 2003, more than 30 percent of the total NTFP firms in the State manufactured specialty wood products, and about 15 percent manufactured culinary items from forest-harvested resources. Floral and decorative enterprises accounted for 19 percent of Tennessee's NTFP industry, and landscaping firms that use native plants or plants

Table 20—Total number of distribution of nontimber forest product enterprises in Southern United States as estimated by county extension agents

State	Edible	Specialty wood	Floral and decorative	Landscape	Medicinal	Total	Percentage of total
				number			
Alabama	221	377	378	377	58	1,411	6
Arkansas	224	257	208	120	251	1,060	4
Florida	216	127	182	837	50	1,412	6
Georgia	250	186	384	1,086	68	1,974	8
Kentucky	490	826	562	373	2,670	4,921	19
Louisiana	249	119	94	81	8	551	2
Mississippi	234	252	207	192	15	900	4
North Carolina	526	452	3,283	1,326	770	6,357	25
Oklahoma	275	148	75	65	14	577	2
South Carolina	89	81	145	216	25	556	2
Tennessee	390	794	481	593	314	2,572	10
Texas	438	210	200	196	27	1,071	4
Virginia	239	370	698	376	262	1,945	8
Total all States	3,841	4,199	6,897	5,838	4,532	25,307	
Percentage of total	15	17	27	23	18		

Flowering dogwood (*Cornus florida*).

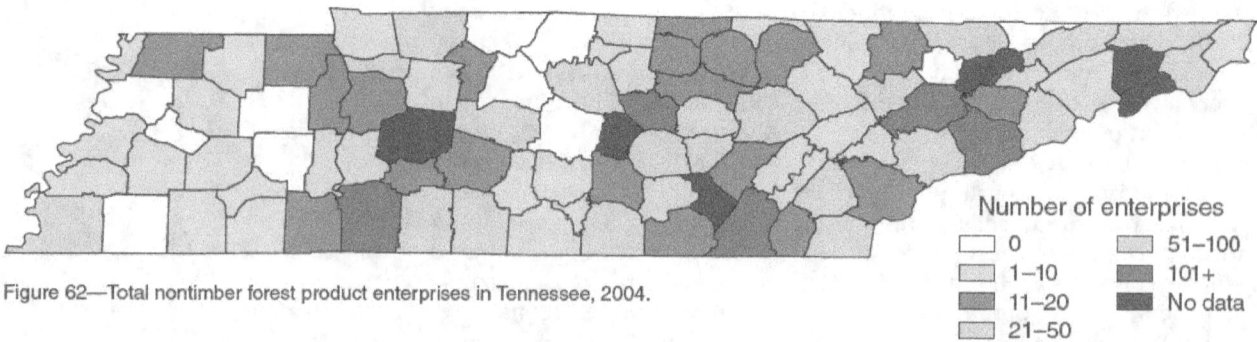

Figure 62—Total nontimber forest product enterprises in Tennessee, 2004.

Number of enterprises

- 0
- 1–10
- 11–20
- 21–50
- 51–100
- 101+
- No data

collected from the wild, accounted for about 23 percent of the industry in the State.

A county level assessment of the 2003 data provides further insight into the distribution of NTFP enterprises (Chamberlain and Predny 2003). Eighty-nine of 95 counties (93.6 percent) reported for this study. Of those, 11 counties (12 percent) reported having no NTFP enterprises. Of the 78 counties that reported having NTFP enterprises, Knox County reported having the most enterprises (510, or about 20 percent). Wayne County ranked second overall with 260 firms (10 percent of the total). Hamilton County, ranked third, reported having 226 firms (almost 9 percent). Sevier (130 firms, or 5 percent), De Kalb (101 firms or 4 percent), and Shelby (78 firms or 3 percent of total). Counties ranked fourth, fifth, and sixth overall, respectively.

There is an enormous selection of medicinal plants growing in the forests of Tennessee and many are harvested for the herbal medicinal industry. Chamberlain (2006) estimates that the Appalachian forests, which are some of the most productive temperate hardwood forests in the world, are the principal source of more than 50 medicinal plant species that are common

to the market. Some of the more popular medicinal plants in the markets today include black cohosh, bloodroot, goldenseal, false unicorn, and slippery elm. Very little information regarding the market value for these plants is available, but that which is gives us valuable insight.

Tennessee is one of six to eight States in the South in which black cohosh and goldenseal have been harvested from State forest land. Evidence suggests that overall demand for black cohosh roots increased from 183,000 pounds in 1999 to more than 500,000 pounds in 2002 (Predny

Lizard's tail
(*Saururus cernuus*).

and others 2006). In 2001, about 420,000 pounds of black cohosh were harvested from forests of the Eastern United States with an estimated market value of about $2.25 million (Predny and Chamberlain 2005). Likewise, in 2000 about 250,000 pounds of goldenseal were demanded, representing a steady market increase (Predny and Chamberlain 2005). Unfortunately, at this time, it is not possible to determine the portion of these harvests that originate from Tennessee's forests. But, if the market dynamics for these and other medicinal plants mirror the market conditions for American ginseng, these plants are significant contributors to rural economies.

Panax quinquefolia (American ginseng) has been dug from eastern hardwood forests since the mid-1700s, and Tennessee has been a major producer for much of the last 300 years (Predny and others 2006). About 70 percent of the total wild-harvested ginseng originates from Tennessee, Kentucky, West Virginia, North Carolina, Indiana, and Virginia. During the period 1979–2005, more than 378,000 pounds of ginseng were harvested from Tennessee forests (fig. 63), generating in excess of $75.6 million in payments to harvesters.

The Cherokee National Forest in Tennessee is a source for many nontimber products. The national forest generates revenues from the sale of permits that allow people to collect these products. In 2004, national forests in Region 8 (Southern Region) generated about $169,000 from permit sales. Tennessee generated $8,858.55 from permit sales and ranked fourth in the region. This revenue came from a variety

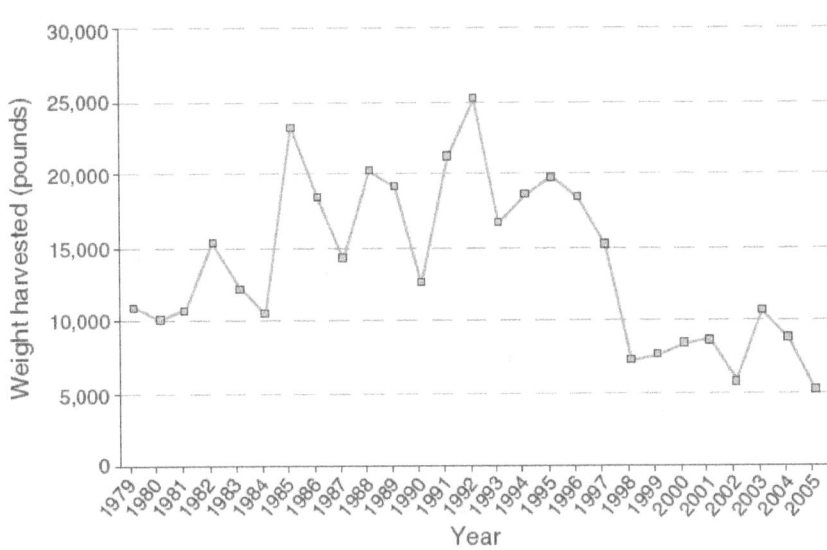

Figure 63—Total wild ginseng harvest in Tennessee, 1979–2005. (Source: Tennessee Natural Heritage Program)

of NTFPs, including fuelwood, roots, moss, herbs, and vines. Sixty-six percent ($5,847) of this revenue came from the sale of permits to harvest transplants used in landscaping with native plants. The collection of roots, perhaps for medicinal purposes, generated about 18 percent ($1,600) of the total revenue. Permits to harvest fuelwood accounted for about 10 percent ($971.55) of total revenues for nontimber products. The sale of permits for herbs, vines, foliage, and seeds and nuts

Sagittaria spp. common to forested wetlands in west Tennessee.

generated about 6 percent ($440) of the NTFP revenues. The general perception among NTFP experts is that revenues from the sale of permits represent about 10 percent of actual market value. This suggests that permitted removal of NTFPs from the Cherokee National Forest potentially had a market value of more than $88,000, which probably is a very conservative estimate. Market valuation for most NTFPs is not fully developed, and there is no way of knowing how much is taken off the forest without permits.

Floral and decorative products include Christmas trees, vines, foliage, moss, needles, limbs, and boughs, as well as cones. Unfortunately, data for most of these are lacking. Christmas trees are the only floral and decorative product with data readily available. The 2002 Census revealed that Tennessee had 186 Christmas tree farms, of which 171 were harvesting trees. More than 2,100 acres of productive farm land were dedicated to Christmas tree production. In 2002, Tennessee produced almost 4 percent (149,770) of the total number of Christmas trees harvested in the South.

Clearly, Tennessee has a vibrant and dynamic NTFP industry. The information presented in this report provides only a partial representation of the industry in the State. The available data indicate that the NTFP industry is a significant contributor to Tennessee's rural economy. Collection and sale of NTFPs directly impact tens of thousands of residents. Getting a more comprehensive, accurate, and reliable portrayal of the NTFP industry would require substantial investment. Such assessment would provide a more complete valuation of these important resources, as well as the forest overall.

The view from Horse Hitch Gap on the Cherokee National Forest in east Tennessee.

American Society for Quality Control. 1994. American national standard: specifications and guidelines for quality systems for environmental data collection and environmental technology programs. ANSI/ASQC E4–1994. Milwaukee, WI: American Society for Quality Control, Energy and Environmental Quality Division, Environmental Issues Group. 32 p.

Barnes, B.V.; Zak, D.R.; Denton, S.R.; Spurr, S.H. 1998. Forest ecology. 4th ed. New York: John Wiley. 774 p.

Baskin, J.M.; Baskin, C.C. 2003. The vascular flora of cedar glades of the Southeastern United States and its phytogeographical relationships. The Journal of the Torrey Botanical Society. 130(2): 101–118.

Bate, L.J.; Torgersen, T.R.; Wisdom, M.J.; Garton, E.O. 2004. Performance of sampling methods to estimate log characteristics for wildlife. Forest Ecology and Management. 199(1): 83–102.

Bechtold, W.R.; Hoffard, W.H.; Anderson, R.L. 1992. Summary report: forest health monitoring in the South, 1991. Gen. Tech. Rep. SE–81. Asheville, NC: U.S. Department of Agriculture Forest Service, Southeastern Forest Experiment Station. 40 p.

Beers, T.W.; Miller, C.L. 1964. Point sampling: research results, theory, and applications. Res. Bull. 786. West Lafayette, IN: Purdue University Agricultural Experiment Station. 56 p.

Butler, B.J.; Leatherberry, E.C.; Williams, M.S. 2005. Design, implementation, and analysis methods for the National Woodland Owner Survey. Gen. Tech. Rep. NE–336. Newtown Square, PA: U.S. Department of Agriculture Forest Service, Northeastern Research Station. 43 p.

Butry, D.T.; Mercer, D.E.; Prestemon, J.P. [and others]. 2001. What is the price of catastrophic wildfire? Journal of Forestry. 99(11): 9–17.

Cassidy, P.D. 2005. A southern pine management guide for Tennessee landowners. PB1751. Knoxville, TN: The University of Tennessee Extension. 47 p.

Chamberlain, J.L. 2006. Conserving the Appalachian medicinal plant industry. In: Morales, M.; Foster, J., eds. Appalachian opportunities: medicinal and aromatic plants: Proceedings, fourth annual symposium on medicinal and aromatic plants: producing, using and marketing herbs and non-timber forest products. Beckley, WV: Mountain State University; 5–15.

Chamberlain, J.L.; Predny, M. 2003. Non-timber forest products enterprises in the South: perceived distribution and implications for sustainable forest management. In: Miller, J.E.; Midtbo, J.M., eds. Proceedings, first national symposium on sustainable natural resource-based alternative enterprises. Mississippi State, MS: Mississippi State University; 48–63.

Coulston, J.W. 2008. Forest inventory and stratified estimation: a cautionary note. Res. Note SRS–RN–16. Asheville, NC: U.S. Department of Agriculture Forest Service, Southern Research Station. 6 p.

Coulston, J.W.; Smith, G.C.; Smith, W.D. 2003. Regional assessment of ozone sensitive tree species using bioindicator plants. Environmental Monitoring and Assessment. 83: 113–127.

Hanks, L.F. 1976. Hardwood tree grades for factory lumber. Res. Pap. NE–333. Broomall, PA: U.S. Department of Agriculture Forest Service, Northeastern Forest Experiment Station. 81 p.

Homer, C.; Dewitz, J.; Fry, J. [and others]. 2007. Completion of the 2001 national land cover database for the Conterminous United States. Photogrammetric Engineering and Remote Sensing. 73(4): 337–341.

Lefohn, A.S.; Jackson, W.; Shadwick, D.S.; Knudsen, H.P. 1997. Effect of surface ozone exposures on vegetation grown in the southern Appalachian Mountains: identification of possible areas of concern. Atmospheric Environments. 31(11): 1695–1708.

Little, E.L., Jr. 1979. Checklist of United States trees (native and naturalized). Agric. Handb. 541. Washington, DC: U.S. Department of Agriculture. 375 p.

Mannan, R.W.; Conner, R.N.; Marcot, B.; Peek, J.M. 1996. Managing forest lands for wildlife. In: Bookhout, T.A., ed. Research and management techniques for wildlife and habitats. Bethesda, MD: The Wildlife Society: 689–721.

McCune, B. 2000. Lichen communities as indicators of forest health. The Bryologist. 103(2): 353–356.

McMahon, C.K. 1983. Characteristics of forest fuels, fires and emissions. In: 76th annual meeting of air pollution control association. Atlanta, GA: 24 p.

Millers, I.; Anderson, R.; Burkman, W.; Hoffard, W. 1992. Crown condition rating guide. Newtown Square, PA: U.S. Department of Agriculture Forest Service, Northeastern Area State and Private Forestry; Atlanta: U.S. Department of Agriculture Forest Service, Southern Region. 37 p.

Millers, I.; Shriner, D.; Rizzo, D. 1989. History of hardwood decline in the Eastern United States. Gen. Tech. Rep. NE–126. Radnor, PA: U.S. Department of Agriculture Forest Service, Northeastern Forest Experiment Station. 75 p.

National Oceanic and Atmospheric Administration (NOAA). 2003. Veterans Day weekend tornado outbreak of November 9-11, 2002. Silver Spring, MD: U.S. Department of Commerce, National Oceanic and Atmospheric Administration. 49 p.

Oswalt, C.M.; Oswalt, S.N.; Clatterbuck, W.K. 2007. Effects of *Microstegium vimineum* (Trin.) A. Camus on native woody species density and diversity in a productive mixed-hardwood forest in Tennessee. Forest Ecology and Management. 242: 727–732.

Predny, M.L.; Chamberlain, J.L. 2005. Goldenseal (*Hydrastis canadensis*): an annotated bibliography. Gen. Tech. Rep. SRS–88. Asheville, NC: U.S. Department of Agriculture Forest Service, Southern Research Station. 67 p.

Predny, M.L.; De Angelis, P.; Chamberlain, J.L. 2006. Black cohosh (*Actaea racemosa*): an annotated bibliography. Gen. Tech. Rep. SRS–97. Asheville, NC: U.S. Department of Agriculture Forest Service, Southern Research Station. 99 p.

Reams G.A.; Smith, W.D.; Hansen, M.H. [and others]. 2005. The forest inventory and analysis sampling frame. In: Bechtold, W.A.; Patterson, P.L., eds. The enhanced forest inventory and analysis program—national sampling design and estimation procedures. Gen. Tech. Rep. SRS–80. Asheville, NC: U.S. Department of Agriculture Forest Service, Southern Research Station: 11–26.

Riitters, K.H.; Wickham, J.D.; O'Neill, R.V. [and others]. 2002. Fragmentation of Continental United States forests. Ecosystems. 5: 815–822.

Schomaker, M.E.; Zarnoch, S.J.; Bechtold, W.A. [and others]. 2007. Crown-condition classification: a guide to data collection and analysis. Gen. Tech. Rep. SRS–102. Asheville, NC: U.S. Department of Agriculture Forest Service, Southern Research Station. 78 p.

Schulz, B. 2003. Changes in downed and dead woody material following a spruce beetle outbreak on the Kenai Peninsula, Alaska. Res. Pap. PNW–RP–559. Portland, OR: U.S. Department of Agriculture Forest Service, Pacific Northwest Research Station. 9 p.

Schweitzer, C.J. 2001. Forest statistics for Tennessee, 1999. Resour. Bull. SRS–52. Asheville, NC: U.S. Department of Agriculture Forest Service, Southern Research Station. 78 p.

Skelly, J.M. 2000. Tropospheric ozone and its importance to forests and natural plant communities of the Northeastern United States. Northeastern Naturalist. 7(3): 221–236.

Smith, G.C.; Smith, W.D.; Coulston, J.W. 2007. Ozone bioindicator sampling and estimation. Gen. Tech. Rep. NRS–20. Newtown Square, PA: U.S. Department of Agriculture Forest Service, Northern Research Station. 34 p.

U.S. Department of Agriculture. 2004a. National report on sustainable forests—2003. For. Serv. Publ. FS–766. Washington, DC: U.S. Department of Agriculture Forest Service, Washington Office. 139 p.

U.S. Department of Agriculture Forest Service. 2004b. White paper, forest products marketing and utilization report. U.S. Department of Agriculture Forest Service, Region 8, State and Private Forestry Technology Marketing Unit Forest Products Laboratory, and Southern Group of State Foresters. Unpublished report. On file with: Southern Research Station, Forest Inventory and Analysis, 4700 Old Kingston Pike, Knoxville, TN 37919.

U.S. Department of Agriculture. 2004c. Field instructions for southern forest inventory. Unpublished report. On file with: Southern Research Station, Forest Inventory and Analysis, 4700 Old Kingston Pike, Knoxville, TN 37919.

U.S. Department of Commerce, Bureau of the Census. 2005. The annual survey of manufacturers, 2004. http://www.factfinder.census.gov. [Date accessed: June 2007]

Waddell, K.L. 2002. Sampling coarse woody debris for multiple attributes in extensive resource inventories. Ecological Indicators. 1(3): 139–153.

Zarnoch, S.J.; Turner, J.A. 2005. Adjustments to forest inventory and analysis estimates of 2001 saw-log volumes for Kentucky. Res. Pap. SRS–38. Asheville, NC: U.S. Department of Agriculture Forest Service, Southern Research Station. 4 p.

The forests along the shoreline of the Tennessee river offer excellent forested habitat for wildlife and plenty of recreational opportunities.

Afforestation. Area of land previously classified as nonforest that is converted to forest by planting of trees or by natural reversion to forest.

Average annual mortality. Average annual volume of trees ≥ 5.0 inches d.b.h. that died from natural causes during the intersurvey period.

Average annual removals. Average annual volume of trees ≥ 5.0 inches d.b.h. removed from the inventory by harvesting, cultural operations (such as timber-stand improvement), land clearing, or changes in land use during the intersurvey period.

Average net annual growth. Average annual net change in volume of trees ≥ 5.0 inches d.b.h. in the absence of cutting (gross growth minus mortality) during the intersurvey period.

Basal area. The area in square feet of the cross section at breast height of a single tree or of all the trees in a stand, usually expressed in square feet per acre.

Bioindicator species. A tree, woody shrub, or nonwoody herb species that responds to ambient levels of ozone pollution with distinctive visible foliar symptoms.

Biomass. The aboveground fresh weight of solid wood and bark in live trees ≥1.0 inch d.b.h. from the ground to the tip of the tree. All foliage is excluded. The weight of wood and bark in lateral limbs, secondary limbs, and twigs < 0.5 inch in diameter at the point of occurrence on sapling-size trees is included but is excluded on poletimber and sawtimber-size trees.

Blind check. A remeasurement done by a qualified inspection crew without production crew data on hand; a full remeasurement of the plot is recommended for the purpose of obtaining a measure of data quality. If a full plot remeasurement is not possible, then it is strongly recommended that at least two full subplots be completely remeasured along with all the plot level information. The two data sets are maintained separately. Discrepancies between the two sets of data are not reconciled. Blind checks are done on production plots only. This procedure provides a quality assessment and evaluation function. The statistics band recommends a random subset of plots be chosen for remeasurement.

Bole. That portion of a tree between a 1-foot stump and a 4-inch top d.o.b. in trees ≥ 5.0 inches d.b.h.

Census water. Streams, sloughs, estuaries, canals, and other moving bodies of water ≥ 200 feet wide, and lakes, reservoirs, ponds, and other permanent bodies of water ≥ 4.5 acres in area.

Coarse woody debris or coarse woody material. Down pieces of wood leaning more than 45 degrees from vertical with a diameter of at least 3.0 inches and a length of at least 3.0 feet (decay classes 1 through 4). Decay class 5 pieces must be at least 5.0 inches in diameter, at least 5.0 inches high from the ground, and at least 3.0 feet in length.

Cold check. An inspection done either as part of the training process, or as part of the ongoing QC program. Normally the installation crew is not present at the time of inspection. The inspector has the completed data in hand at the time of inspection. The inspection can include the whole plot or a subset of the plot. Data errors are corrected. Cold checks are done on production plots only. This type of quality control measurement is a "blind" measurement in that the crews do not know when or which of their plots will be remeasured by the inspection crew and cannot therefore alter their performance because of knowledge that the plot is a QA plot.

Compacted area. Type of compaction measured as part of the soil indicator. Examples include the junction areas of skid trails, landing areas, work areas, etc.

Condition class. The combination of discrete landscape and forest attributes that identify, define, and stratify the area associated with a plot. Examples of such attributes include condition status, forest type, stand origin, stand size, owner group, reserve status, and stand density.

Crown. The part of a tree or woody plant bearing live branches or foliage.

Crown density. The amount of crown stem, branches, twigs, shoots, buds, foliage, and reproductive structures that block light penetration through the visible crown. Dead branches and dead tops are part of the crown. Live and dead branches below the live crown base are excluded. Broken or missing tops are visually reconstructed when forming this crown outline by comparing outlines of adjacent healthy trees of the same species and d.b.h./d.r.c. (root collar diameter).

Crown dieback. This is recent mortality of branches with fine twigs, which begins at the terminal portion of a branch and proceeds toward the trunk. Dieback is only considered when it occurs in the upper and outer portions of the tree. When whole branches are dead in the upper crown, without obvious signs of damage such as breaks or animal injury, assume that the branches died from the terminal portion of the branch. Dead branches in the lower portion of the live crown are assumed to have died from competition and shading. Dead branches in the lower live crown are not considered part of crown dieback, unless there is continuous dieback from the upper and outer crown down to those branches.

D.b.h. Tree diameter in inches (outside bark) at breast height (4.5 feet aboveground).

Decay class. Qualitative assessment of stage of decay (5 classes) of coarse woody debris based on visual assessments of color of wood, presence/absence of twigs and branches, texture of rotten portions, and structural integrity.

Diameter class. A classification of trees based on tree d.b.h. Two-inch diameter classes are commonly used by FIA, with the even inch as the approximate midpoint for a class. For example, the 6-inch class includes trees 5.0–6.9 inches d.b.h.

D.o.b. (diameter outside bark). Stem diameter including bark.

Down woody material (DWM). Woody pieces of trees and shrubs that have been uprooted (no longer supporting growth) or severed from their root system, not self-supporting, and are lying on the ground. Previously named down woody debris (DWD).

Duff. A soil layer dominated by organic material derived from the decomposition of plant and animal litter and deposited on either an organic or a mineral surface. This layer is distinguished from the litter layer in that the original organic material has undergone sufficient decomposition that the source of this material (e.g., individual plant parts) can no longer be identified.

Effective cation exchange capacity (ECEC). The sum of cations that a soil can adsorb in its natural pH. Expressed in units of centimoles of positive charge per kilogram of soil.

Erosion. The wearing away of the land surface by running water, wind, ice, or other geological agents.

Fine woody debris or fine woody material. Down pieces of wood with a diameter < 3.0 inches, not including foliage or bark fragments.

Foliage transparency. The amount of skylight visible through micro-holes in the live portion of the crown (i.e., where you see foliage, normal or damaged, or remnants of its recent presence). Recently defoliated branches are included in foliage transparency measurements. Macro-holes are excluded unless they are the result of recent defoliation. Dieback and dead branches are always excluded from the estimate. Foliage transparency is different from crown density because it emphasizes foliage and ignores stems, branches, fruits, and holes in the crown.

Forest floor. The entire thickness of organic material overlying the mineral soil, consisting of the litter and the duff (humus).

Forest land. Land at least 10 percent stocked by forest trees of any size, or formerly having had such tree cover, and not currently developed for nonforest use. The minimum area considered for classification is 1 acre. Forested strips must be at least 120 feet wide.

Forest management type. A classification of timberland based on forest type and stand origin.

Pine plantation. Stands that (1) have been artificially regenerated by planting or direct seeding, (2) are classed as a pine or other softwood forest type, and (3) have at least 10 percent stocking.

Natural pine. Stands that (1) have not been artificially regenerated, (2) are classed as a pine or other softwood forest type, and (3) have at least 10 percent stocking.

Oak-pine. Stands that have at least 10 percent stocking and classed as a forest type of oak-pine.

Upland hardwood. Stands that have at least 10 percent stocking and classed as an oak-hickory or maple-beech-birch forest type.

Lowland hardwood. Stands that have at least 10 percent stocking with a forest type of oak-gum-cypress, elm-ash-cottonwood, palm, or other tropical.

Nonstocked stands. Stands < 10 percent stocked with live trees.

Forest type. A classification of forest land based on the species forming a plurality of live-tree stocking. Major eastern forest-type groups are:

White-red-jack pine. Forests in which eastern white pine, red pine, or jack pine, singly or in combination, constitute a plurality of the stocking. (Common associates include hemlock, birch, and maple.)

Spruce-fir. Forests in which spruce or true firs, singly or in combination, constitute a plurality of the stocking. (Common associates include maple, birch, and hemlock.)

Longleaf-slash pine. Forests in which longleaf or slash pine, singly or in combination, constitute a plurality of the stocking. (Common associates include oak, hickory, and gum.)

Loblolly-shortleaf pine. Forests in which loblolly pine, shortleaf pine, or other southern yellow pines, except longleaf or slash pine, singly or in combination, constitute a plurality of the stocking. (Common associates include oak, hickory, and gum.)

Oak-pine. Forests in which hardwoods (usually upland oaks) constitute a plurality of the stocking but in which pines account for 25 to 50 percent of the stocking. (Common associates include gum, hickory, and yellow-poplar.)

Oak-hickory. Forests in which upland oaks or hickory, singly or in combination, constitute a plurality of the stocking, except where pines account for 25 to 50 percent, in which case the stand would be classified oak-pine. (Common associates include yellow-poplar, elm, maple, and black walnut.)

Oak-gum-cypress. Bottomland forests in which tupelo, blackgum, sweetgum, oaks, or southern cypress, singly or in combination, constitute a plurality of the stocking, except where pines account for 25 to 50 percent of stocking, in which case the stand would be classified as oak-pine. (Common associates include cottonwood, willow, ash, elm, hackberry, and maple.)

Elm-ash-cottonwood. Forests in which elm, ash, or cottonwood, singly or in combination, constitute a plurality of the stocking. (Common associates include willow, sycamore, beech, and maple.)

Maple-beech-birch. Forests in which maple, beech, or yellow birch, singly or in combination, constitute a plurality of the stocking. (Common associates include hemlock, elm, basswood, and white pine.)

Nonstocked stands. Stands < 10 percent stocked with live trees.

Forested tract size. The area of forest within the contiguous tract containing each FIA sample plot.

Fresh weight. Mass of tree component at time of cutting.

Fuel bed. Accumulated mass of all DWM components above the top of the duff layer. The fuel bed does not include live shrubs or herbs.

Fuel hour classes. Fuel classes defined by the approximate amount of time it takes for moisture conditions to fluctuate. Larger coarse woody material will takes longer to dry out than smaller fine woody pieces (Small = 1-hour, Medium = 10-hour, Large = 100-hour, Coarse woody material = 1,000-hour).

Gross growth. Annual increase in volume of trees ≥ 5.0 inches d.b.h. in the absence of cutting and mortality. (Gross growth includes survivor growth, ingrowth, growth on ingrowth, growth on removals before removal, and growth on mortality before death.)

Growing-stock trees. Living trees of commercial species classified as sawtimber, poletimber, saplings, and seedlings. Trees must contain at least one 12-foot or two 8-foot logs in the saw-log portion, currently or potentially (if too small to qualify), to be classed as growing stock. The log(s) must meet dimension and merchantability standards to qualify. Trees must also have, currently or potentially, one-third of the gross board-foot volume in sound wood.

Growing-stock volume. The cubic-foot volume of sound wood in growing-stock trees ≥ 5.0 inches d.b.h. from a 1-foot stump to a minimum 4.0-inch top d.o.b. of the central stem.

Hardwoods. Dicotyledonous trees, usually broadleaf and deciduous.

Soft hardwoods. Hardwood species with an average specific gravity of ≤ 0.50, such as gums, yellow-poplar, cottonwoods, red maple, basswoods, and willows.

Hard hardwoods. Hardwood species with an average specific gravity > 0.50, such as oaks, hard maples, hickories, and beech.

Hexagonal grid (Hex). A hexagonal grid formed from equilateral triangles for the purpose of tessellating the FIA inventory sample. Each hexagon in the base grid has an area of 5,937 acres (2,403.6 ha) and contains one inventory plot. The base grid can be subdivided into smaller hexagons to intensify the sample.

Humus. A soil layer dominated by organic material derived from the decomposition of plant and animal litter and deposited on either an organic or a mineral surface. This layer is distinguished from the litter layer in that the original organic material has undergone sufficient decomposition that the source of this material (e.g., individual plant parts) can no longer be identified.

Land area. The area of dry land and land temporarily or partly covered by water, such as marshes, swamps, and river floodplains (omitting tidal flats below mean high tide), streams, sloughs, estuaries, and canals < 200 feet wide, and lakes, reservoirs, and ponds < 4.5 acres in area.

Lichen. An organism generally appearing to be a single small leafy, tufted or crust-like plant that consists of a fungus and an alga or cyanobacterium living in symbiotic association.

Lichen community indicator. The set of macrolichen species collected on a FIA lichen plot using standard protocols, which serves as an indicator of ecological condition (e.g., air quality or climate) of the plot.

Lichen plot. The FIA lichen plot is a circular area, total 0.935 acre (0.4 ha), with a 120 foot (36.6 m) radius centered on subplot 1, and excluding the 4 subplots.

Litter. Undecomposed or only partially decomposed organic material that can be readily identified (e.g., plant leaves, twigs, etc.).

Live trees. All living trees. All size classes, all tree classes, and both commercial and noncommercial species are included.

Measurement quality objective (MQO). A data user's estimate of the precision, bias, and completeness of data necessary to satisfy a prescribed application (e.g., Resource Planning Act (RPA), assessments by State foresters, forest planning, forest health analyses). Describes the acceptable tolerance for each data element. MQOs consist of two parts: a statement of the tolerance and a percentage of time when the collected data are required to be within tolerance. Measurement quality objectives can only be assigned where standard methods of sampling or field measurements exist, or where experience has established upper or lower bounds on precision or bias. Measurement quality objectives can be set for measured data elements, observed data elements, and derived data elements.

Mineral soil. A soil consisting predominantly of products derived from the weathering of rocks (e.g., sands, silts, and clays).

Net annual change. Increase or decrease in volume of live trees ≥ 5.0 inches d.b.h. Net annual change is equal to net annual growth minus average annual removals.

Noncommercial species. Tree species of typically small size, poor form, or inferior quality that normally do not develop into trees suitable for industrial wood products.

Nonforest land. Land that has never supported forests and land formerly forested where timber production is precluded by development for other uses.

Nonstocked stands. Stands < 10 percent stocked with live trees.

Other forest land. Forest land other than timberland and productive reserved forest land. It includes available and reserved forest land which is incapable of producing annually 20 cubic feet per acre of industrial wood under natural conditions, because of adverse site conditions such as sterile soils, dry climate, poor drainage, high elevation, steepness, or rockiness.

Other removals. The growing-stock volume of trees removed from the inventory by cultural operations such as timber stand improvement, land clearing, and other changes in land use, resulting in the removal of the trees from timberland.

Ozone. O_3. A gaseous air pollutant produced primarily through sunlight-driven chemical reactions of NO_2 and hydrocarbons in the atmosphere and causing foliar injury to deciduous trees, conifers, shrubs, and herbaceous species.

Ozone bioindicator site. An open area in which ozone injury to ozone-sensitive species is evaluated. The area must meet certain site selection guidelines regarding size, condition, and plant counts to be used for ozone injury evaluations in FIA.

Ownership. The property owned by one ownership unit, including all parcels of land in the United States.

National forest land. Federal land that has been legally designated as national forests or purchase units, and other land under the administration of the Forest Service, including experimental areas and Bankhead-Jones Title III land.

Forest industry land. Land owned by companies or individuals operating primary wood-using plants.

Nonindustrial private forest land. Privately owned land excluding forest industry land.

Corporate. Owned by corporations, including incorporated farm ownerships.

Individual. All lands owned by individuals, including farm operators.

Other public. An ownership class that includes all public lands except national forests.

Miscellaneous Federal land. Federal land other than national forests.

State, county, and municipal land. Land owned by States, counties, and local public agencies or municipalities or land leased to these governmental units for ≥ 50 years.

Phase 1 (P1). FIA activities related to remote-sensing, the primary purpose of which is to label plots and obtain stratum weights for population estimates.

Phase 2 (P2). FIA activities conducted on the network of ground plots. The primary purpose is to obtain field data that enable classification and summarization of area, tree, and other attributes associated with forest land uses.

Phase 3 (P3). FIA activities conducted on a subset of Phase 2 plots. Additional attributes related to forest health are measured on Phase 3 plots.

Poletimber-size trees. Softwoods 5.0 to 8.9 inches d.b.h. and hardwoods 5.0–10.9 inches d.b.h.

Productive-reserved forest land. Forest land sufficiently productive to qualify as timberland but withdrawn from timber utilization through statute or administrative regulation.

Quality assurance (QA). The total integrated program for ensuring that the uncertainties inherent in FIA data are known and do not exceed acceptable magnitudes, within a stated level of confidence. Quality assurance encompasses the plans, specifications, and policies affecting the collection, processing, and reporting of data. It is the system of activities designed to provide program managers and project leaders with independent assurance that total system quality control is being effectively implemented.

Quality control (QC). The routine application of prescribed field and laboratory procedures (e.g., random check cruising, periodic calibration, instrument maintenance, use of certified standards, etc.) in order to reduce random and systematic errors and ensure that data are generated within known and acceptable performance limits. Quality control also ensures the use of qualified personnel; reliable equipment and supplies; training of personnel; good field and laboratory practices; and strict adherence to standard operating procedures.

Reforestation. Area of land previously classified as forest that is regenerated by tree planting or natural regeneration.

Rotten trees. Live trees of commercial species not containing at least one 12-foot saw log, or two noncontiguous saw logs, each ≥ 8 feet, now or prospectively, primarily because of rot or missing sections, and with less than one-third of the gross board-foot tree volume in sound material.

Rough trees. Live trees of commercial species not containing at least one 12-foot saw log, or two noncontiguous saw logs, each ≥ 8 feet, now or prospectively, primarily because of roughness, poor form, splits, and cracks, and with less than one-third of the gross board-foot tree volume in sound material; and live trees of noncommercial species.

Sapling. Live trees 1.0 to 4.9 inches (2.5 to 12.5 cm) in diameter (d.b.h.).

Saw log. A log meeting minimum standards of diameter, length, and defect, including logs ≥ 8 feet long, sound and straight, with a minimum diameter inside bark for softwoods of 6 inches (8 inches for hardwoods).

Saw-log portion. The part of the bole of sawtimber trees between a 1-foot stump and the saw-log top.

Saw-log top. The point on the bole of sawtimber trees above which a conventional saw log cannot be produced. The minimum saw-log top is 7.0 inches d.o.b. for softwoods and 9.0 inches d.o.b. for hardwoods.

Sawtimber-size trees. Softwoods ≥ 9.0 inches d.b.h. and hardwoods ≥ 11.0 inches d.b.h..

Sawtimber volume. Growing-stock volume in the saw-log portion of sawtimber-size trees in board feet (International 1/4-inch rule).

Seedlings. Trees < 1.0 inch d.b.h. and > 1 foot tall for hardwoods, > 6 inches tall for softwoods, and > 0.5 inch in diameter at ground level for longleaf pine.

Select red oaks. A group of several red oak species composed of cherrybark, Shumard, and northern red oaks. Other red oak species are included in the "other red oaks" group.

Select white oaks. A group of several white oak species composed of white, swamp chestnut, swamp white, chinkapin, Durand, and bur oaks. Other white oak species are included in the "other white oaks" group.

Site class. A classification of forest land in terms of potential capacity to grow crops of industrial wood based on fully stocked natural stands.

Softwoods. Coniferous trees, usually evergreen, having leaves that are needles or scalelike.

Yellow pines. Loblolly, longleaf, slash, pond, shortleaf, pitch, Virginia, sand, spruce, and Table Mountain pines.

Other softwoods. Cypress, eastern redcedar, white-cedar, eastern white pine, eastern hemlock, spruce, and fir.

Soil bulk density. The mass of soil per unit volume. A measure of the ratio of pore space to solid materials in a given soil. Expressed in grams per cubic cm of oven dry soil.

Soil compaction. A reduction in soil pore space caused by heavy equipment or by repeated passes of light equipment that compress the soil and break down soil aggregates. Compaction disturbs the soil structure and can cause decreased tree growth, increased water runoff, and soil erosion.

Soil texture. The relative proportions of sand, silt, and clay in a soil.

Stand age. The average age of dominant and codominant trees in the stand.

Stand origin. A classification of forest stands describing their means of origin.

Planted. Planted or artificially seeded.

Natural. No evidence of artificial regeneration.

Stand-size class. A classification of forest land based on the diameter class distribution of live trees in the stand.

Sawtimber stands. Stands at least 10 percent stocked with live trees, with one-half or more of total stocking in sawtimber and poletimber trees, and with sawtimber stocking at least equal to poletimber stocking.

Poletimber stands. Stands at least 10 percent stocked with live trees, with one-half or more of total stocking in poletimber and sawtimber trees, and with poletimber stocking exceeding sawtimber stocking.

Sapling-seedling stands. Stands at least 10 percent stocked with live trees, in which saplings and seedlings account for more than one-half of total stocking.

Nonstocked stands. Stands < 10 percent stocked with live trees.

Stocking. The degree of occupancy of land by trees, measured by basal area or the number of trees in a stand and spacing in the stand, compared with a minimum standard, depending on tree size, required to fully utilize the growth potential of the land.

Density of live trees and basal area per acre required for full stocking:

D.b.h. class	Trees per acre for full stocking	Basal area
inches		*square feet per acre*
Seedlings (< 1 inch)	600	—
2	560	—
4	460	—
6	340	67
8	240	84
10	155	85
12	115	90
14	90	96
16	72	101
18	60	106
20	51	111

— = not applicable.

Timberland. Forest land capable of producing 20 cubic feet of industrial wood per acre per year and not withdrawn from timber utilization.

Transect diameter. Diameter of a coarse woody piece at the point of intersection with a sampling plane.

Tree. Woody plant having one erect perennial stem or trunk ≥ 3 inches d.b.h., a more or less definitely formed crown of foliage, and a height of ≥ 13 feet (at maturity).

Tree grade. A classification of the saw-log portion of sawtimber trees based on: (1) the grade of the butt log or (2) the ability to produce at least one 12-foot or two 8-foot logs in the upper section of the saw-log portion. Tree grade is an indicator of quality; grade 1 is the best quality.

Upper-stem portion. The part of the main stem or fork of sawtimber trees above the saw-log top to a minimum top diameter of 4.0 inches outside bark or to the point where the main stem or fork breaks into limbs.

Vigor class. A visual assessment of the apparent crown vigor of saplings. The purpose is to separate excellent saplings with superior crowns from stressed individuals with poor crowns.

Volume of live trees. The cubic-foot volume of sound wood in live trees ≥ 5.0 inches d.b.h. from a 1-foot stump to a minimum 4.0-inch top d.o.b. of the central stem.

Volume of saw-log portion of sawtimber trees. The cubic-foot volume of sound wood in the saw-log portion of sawtimber trees. Volume is the net result after deductions for rot, sweep, and other defects that affect use for lumber.

The fall foliage of blackgum (*Nyssa aquatica*) makes for a fantastic display of color in many eastern forests.

Forest Inventory Methods

A State-by-State inventory of the Nation's forest land began in the mid-1930s. These surveys primarily were designed and conducted to provide estimates of forest area, wood volume, tree growth, removals, and mortality. Throughout the years, numerous technical innovations and national concerns over perceived and real trends in forest resource conditions have led to many improvements (Reams and others 2005). The primary purpose for conducting forest inventories has remained unchanged, but the methods have undergone substantial change. The following is a general description of the current sample design used to collect the information and procedures used to derive the forest resource estimates provided in this report. A brief discussion of past sample designs and procedures is included to alert users to substantive changes.

The seventh survey of Tennessee's forest resources marks a shift in design, intensity, and timeliness of data collection. The Agricultural Research Extension and Education Reform Act of 1998 (Farm Bill) mandated annual surveys of U.S. forests.

The annual surveys feature: (1) a nationally consistent, fixed-radius, four-point plot configuration; (2) a systematic national sampling design consisting of a base grid of approximately 6,000-acre hexagons; (3) integration of the forest inventory and forest health monitoring sample designs; (4) annual measurement of a fixed proportion of permanent plots across the State; (5) reporting of data or data summaries within 6 months after yearly sampling; (6) an annual estimator based on a default 5-year moving average, with provisions for optional estimators based on techniques for updating information; and (7) a summary report every 5 years. Additional information about annual surveys is available at www.fia.fs.fed.us.

The current inventory is a 3-phase, fixed-plot sample design conducted on an annual basis. Phase 1 (P1) provides the forest land area estimates for the inventory. Phase 2 (P2) involves on the ground measurements of sample plots by field personnel. Phase 3 (P3) is a subset of the P2 plot system where additional measurements are made by field personnel to assess forest health indicators. The three phases of the current sampling method are based on a hexagonal-grid design (fig. A.1). There are about 25 P1 points for

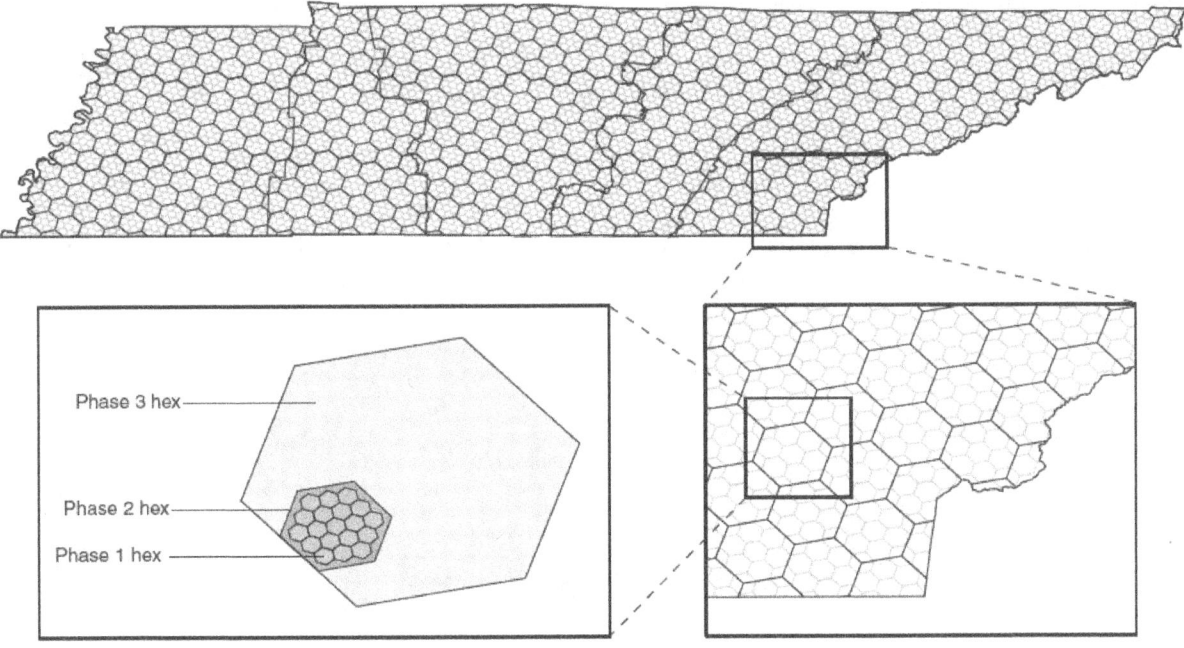

Figure A.1—The FIA hexagonal grid system for locating phase 1, 2, and 3 plots in Tennessee.

every P2 plot. There are 16 P2 plots for every P3 plot. P1 points and P2 and 3 plots represent about 222 acres, 6,000 acres, and 96,000 acres each, respectively.

The inventory design and methodology used to collect and process the information needed to derive the current forest resource estimates for the 2004 survey of Tennessee have undergone change since the previous survey conducted in 1999. The 2004 survey's sample design has changed in three major ways from the previous inventory of Tennessee. The first change was in the method of collecting forest area estimation. Secondly, the temporal nature of collecting the ground samples switched from a periodic survey to an annual survey. There are also changes in volume equations, variable definitions, processing methodology, and algorithms. While all of these changes, alone or in combination, weaken comparisons among surveys, they are necessary to improve upon survey accuracy and allow comparisons with other surveys throughout the region, the entire continental United States, and the world. A clear understanding of these changes is necessary when making rigorous comparisons among inventories.

Previous Sample Design

Prior to the 2004 inventory, the Southern Research Station Forest Inventory and Analysis (FIA) Program secured data on forest acreage and timber volume using a three-step process. A forest-nonforest classification using aerial photographs was accomplished for points representing about

230 acres. These photo classifications were adjusted based on ground observations at sample locations representing about 3,840 acres. Finally, field measurements were made at forest locations on the intersections of grid lines spaced 3 miles apart.

Ownership information was collected for any plot location where all or a portion of the plot sampled forest land. Ownership data were collected for individual counties using information from county courthouse records. Confirmations of owners were made when needed by direct contact. National forest lands and State-owned lands for each county were enumerated by office personnel.

The plot design at each ground sample location was based on a cluster of four points spaced 120 feet apart (fig. A.2). Each point served as the center of a 1/24-acre circular subplot used to sample trees 5.0-inches diameter at breast height (d.b.h.) and larger. A 1/300-acre circular microplot, located at the center of the subplot, was used to sample trees 1.0- through 4.9-inches d.b.h. and seedlings (trees < 1.0 inches as d.b.h.). These fixed-radius sample plots were established without regard to land use or forest cover. In surveys prior to 1999, points were rotated or moved so that location of points on forested land was maximized. The new design no longer includes this practice.

The cluster of four fixed-area subplots sampled forest land at 2,465 ground sample locations in the State of Tennessee for the 1999 inventory. Estimates of timber volume

and forest classification were derived from tree measurements and classifications made at these locations. Volumes for individual tally trees were computed using equations for each of the major species in the survey unit. The equations were developed from detailed measurements of standing trees in this survey unit and throughout the region. The 1999 survey data were analyzed using volume methodology that is based on the typical D^2H volume equations produced on a species or species group basis using a simple linear regression model with the method of three means. Volume inside bark from a 1.0-foot stump to a 4.0-inch upper diameter outside bark is predicted for each sample tree based on d.b.h. and height and does not include forks or limbs outside the main bole.

Estimates of growth, removals, and mortality were determined from the remeasurement of permanent sample plots established in the previous inventory.

Current Sample Design

Current phase 1: forest area estimates—
Following the 1999 inventory, FIA has now bases the three phases of the current sampling method on a hex-grid design (fig. A.1), with each successive phase sampled with less intensity. There are 16 P2 hexes for every P3 hex, and 27 P1 hexes for every P2 hex. P1 hexes represent about 222 acres, while P2 and P3 hexes represent roughly 6,000 acres and 96,000 acres, respectively.

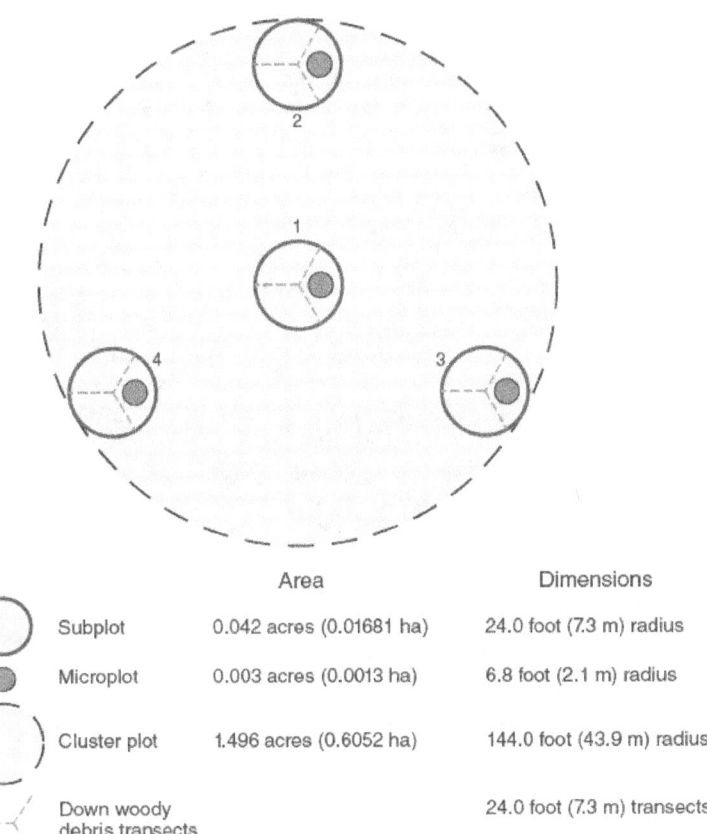

		Area	Dimensions
○	Subplot	0.042 acres (0.01681 ha)	24.0 foot (7.3 m) radius
●	Microplot	0.003 acres (0.0013 ha)	6.8 foot (2.1 m) radius
(⌐)	Cluster plot	1.496 acres (0.6052 ha)	144.0 foot (43.9 m) radius
	Down woody debris transects		24.0 foot (7.3 m) transects

Figure A.2—Layout of annual fixed-radius plot design. The cluster plot is a circle circumscribing the outer edge of the four subplots.

P1 involves assigning a plot to the P1 hexes on digital imagery—currently FIA uses the National Land Cover Database (NLCD). Each hex point, or "dot," is classified as either forest or nonforest and a percentage for each class is derived for the entire State. The P1 point classifications are then checked at permanent ground sample locations that make up the P2 sample. Two correction factors are created by comparing the forest and nonforest classifications on the digital imagery to the classifications of the same points made at ground sample locations. These correction factors are used to adjust the percent forest derived from the original (P1) estimate. These correction factors adjust for possible misclassifications in the NLCD and for change on the ground that occurred since the date of the digital imagery used for land cover classification.

P2 locations generally are not placed in the center of the hex. If a sample location from a prior inventory exists in a P2 hex, then that same location is used again. If two sample locations from a prior survey existed with the same hex, then one is dropped. For P2 hexes containing no prior sample location, a new sample location is created at a random point within the hex. This process is performed in a manner that maintains as many existing plots as possible. While prior surveys used enumeration for selected owner classes, the current survey does not. The areas assigned to various characteristics (e.g., ownership, stand-size, and forest type) are based on the expansion factor assigned and derived in the first phase.

Current phase 2: forest inventory—In the 2004 inventory, the plot design employed a fixed-plot composed of four subplots spaced 120 feet apart (fig. A.2). (*Note: Readers will notice that this is the same plot design used in the 1999 inventory.) The sample area of these four subplots was 1/6 of an acre, while the footprint of the cluster was about 1 acre. Trees ≥ 5.0 inches in d.b.h. were measured on each subplot (1/24 of an acre; 24-foot radius). Trees 1.0–4.9 inches in d.b.h. and seedlings (< 1.0 inches in d.b.h.) were measured on a microplot (1/300 of an acre; 6.8 foot radius) on each of the four subplots. The cluster of four fixed-area subplots sampled forest land at 2,344 ground sample locations.

A unique feature of this plot design was in the mapping of different land use and forest conditions that are encountered on the plot cluster. Because the plots were placed on the ground without bias (i.e., systematically, but at a scale large enough so that placement could be considered random), there was a probability that the plot cluster might straddle more than one type of land use or forest condition. Furthermore, the four subplots were not relocated into the same land use. If a plot happened to straddle multiple land uses and forest conditions, then the crew identified the differences encountered on the plot. There were two steps in the mapping process. The first step involved identifying forest and nonforest areas on the plot and establishing a boundary line on the

plot if both were present. The second step involved identifying differing conditions in the forested portion of the plot based on six factors: (1) forest type, (2) stand size, (3) ownership, (4) stand density, (5) regeneration status, and (6) reserved status. These, too, were mapped into separate entities.

Estimates of growth, removals, and mortality were determined from the remeasurement of 2,127 permanent sample plots established in the previous inventory. Remeasurement information was used in the calculation of seven components of change: (1) survivor growth, (2) ingrowth, (3) growth on ingrowth, (4) mortality, (5) growth on mortality, (6) removals, and (7) growth on removals. Estimates of gross growth, net growth, and net change were made following Beers and Miller (1964).

Phase 3: forest health—In the 2004 inventory, forest health variables (P3) were collected on about 1/16th of the P2 sample plots. P3 data are coarse descriptions and are meant to be used as general indicators of overall forest health over large geographic areas. This data were not collected in Tennessee until 2000, so there is no previous methodology to compare and contrast.

P3 data collection includes variables pertaining to tree crown health, down woody material (DWM), foliar ozone injury, lichen diversity, and soil composition. Tree crown health, DWM, and soil composition measurements were collected using the same plot design used during P2 data collection, while lichen data were collected within a 120-foot radius circle centered on subplot 1 of each FIA P3 field plot.

Biomonitoring sites for ozone data collection were based on specific criteria and were located independently of the FIA grid. Sites chosen were 1-acre fields or similar open areas adjacent to or surrounded by forest land, and contained at least a minimum number of plants of at least two identified bioindicator species (Smith and others 2007). Plants were evaluated for ozone injury, and voucher specimens were submitted to a regional expert for verification of ozone-induced foliar injury.

Bowmans root (*Gillenia trifoliata*).

Annual versus Periodic

Previous surveys of Tennessee were done in a periodic fashion; all of the plots were measured in 1–2 years with remeasurement about every 10 years. The current, annual inventory design was implemented to provide more up-to-date information about forest resources. The goal of the annual inventory system is to measure 20 percent (referred to as a panel or subcycle) of the total plots in the State each year so that all plots are measured within a 5-year period (one cycle). Each year's panel of plots is selected on a subgrid which is slightly offset from the previous year's plots, thus each year covers essentially the same sample area (both spatially and in intensity) as the prior year. In the sixth year the plots that were measured in the first panel are remeasured. This marks the beginning of the next cycle of data collection.

After field measurements are completed, a cycle of data (consisting of data from five panels of plots) is available for a 5-year report. This dataset consists of data collected at different times: 20 percent of the data would be < 1-year-old, 20 percent > 1 but < 2-years-old, and so on.

One of the major impacts on data interpretation and analyses of switching to the annual inventory design is the length of time for data collection (5 years versus 1 or 2 years). Data collected over a longer period of time have a higher probability of sampling a specific event, (e.g., a hurricane or fire), but only on a small proportion of the sample. However, data collected over a shorter time span may miss an event entirely until the next periodic measurement takes place, at which time all of the sample plots reflect the event. This may be further complicated by the number of years passing since the event, before remeasurement occurs.

Accompanying Statistical Tables

The Forest Service, Southern Research Station (SRS) FIA Program has begun publishing a set of accompanying statistical tables online. In an effort to reduce the time needed for formatting, the SRS FIA program is making the tables available online as a supplement to this report. The supplemental tables are representative of many of the tables historically published by FIA and include unit level estimates, estimates

A mixed pine hardwood stand approximately 25 years after a natural wildfire in eastern Tennessee.

of biomass and carbon, and many other Statewide and regional-level estimates. Statistical tables will be available for online viewing and printing at: http://srsfia2.fs.fed.us/states/tennessee. shtml.

If a hard copy is required, or if you cannot access the online tables, please contact the SRS FIA Program at the address below.

Information concerning any aspect of this survey may be obtained from:

Forest Inventory and Analysis
USDA Forest Service
Southern Research Station
4700 Old Kingston Pike
Knoxville, TN 37919
Phone: 865-862-2000

Tabular data included in FIA reports are designed to provide a comprehensive array of forest resources statistics, but additional data can be obtained for those who require more specialized information. The Forest Inventory and Analysis Database (FIADB) for the United States can currently be accessed via the Internet at fia.fs.fed.us/ tools-data. Special requests for FIA data may be submitted to SRS FIA Spatial Data Services, located on the Internet at srsfia2. fs.fed.us/sds/index.shtml. Additional forest resource information for the Southern States is available on the Internet at srsfia2.fs.fed.us.

Changes in Variable Assessments

The methods used to assess various attributes have changed in some cases and this may affect trend analyses. Prior to the 1999 inventory, field personnel evaluated the forested area of the plot as a single stand, using the plurality of stocking as the basis of assessing most of the stand

variables. Procedures for the 1999 inventory and the 2004 inventory require mapping of different forest conditions across the plot, and then recording the differences in stand characteristics. This leads to a change in the size and homogeneity of the assessment areas between inventories. There are also some differences between the 1999 algorithms employed and the algorithms used for the 2004 inventory to compute stocking, stand size, and forest type. As FIA standardizes these algorithms nationally, these differences across regions will diminish.

Privacy Laws

It is important that forest landowners and FIA data users be aware that Federal law requires that private ownership information collected by FIA shall not be made available for public distribution. In addition, Federal law also requires that the exact locations of all FIA plots shall not be made public so that the ownership of each plot could be determined. This report summarizes FIA data by ownership class at the unit and State level. FIA can provide county-level information about the amounts of land in the public and private ownership classes, but more detailed county-level land ownership information is not available from FIA.

Summary

Users wishing to make rigorous comparisons between data obtained in different surveys should be aware of the survey-to-survey differences in plot designs and variable assessments. Assuming there is no bias in plot selection or maintenance of plot integrity, the most valuable and powerful trend information comes from the same plots being revisited from one survey

to the next and measured in the same way. This is also the only method that yields reliable components of change estimation (growth, removals, and mortality). This approach reduces the noise that is present in natural forest stands and lends a higher level of confidence in assessing trends. However, if sample designs change, there can never be a high level of certainty that the trends in the data are real and not the result of procedural changes. Even though both designs may be judged statistically valid, the naturally occurring noise in the data hinders confident and rigorous assessments of trend over time. Defining the confidence and strength of trend over time is difficult when sample methodology changes over time.

Inventory Quality Assurance and Quality Control

The goal of the FIA quality assurance (QA) program is to provide a framework that ensures that forest assessments meet given standards for completeness, accuracy, and absence of bias. This program is organized in accordance with the protocols set forth in part B of the American National Standard for the Quality of Environmental Data collection (American Society for Quality Control 1994). One of the goals of the FIA Program is to include data quality documentation in all nationally available reports, including State reports and national summary reports. This report includes a summary of P2 variables and measurement quality objective (MQO) analyses from FIA blind check measurements. Quality assessments of the P3 data will be addressed in future reports. Quality control (QC)

procedures include feedback to field staff to provide assessment and improvement of crew performance. Additionally, data quality is assessed and documented using performance measurements and post survey assessments. These assessments then are used to identify areas of the data collection process that need improvement or refinement in order to meet quality objectives of the program.

Quality assurance and quality control methods—FIA implements QA methods in several different ways. These methods include nationally standardized field manuals, portable data recorders (PDR), training and certification of field crews, and field audits. The PDRs help ensure that specified procedures are followed. The minimum national standards for annual training of field crews are: (1) a minimum of 40 hours for new employees, and (2) a minimum of 8 hours for return employees. Field crew members are certified via an in-situ test plot. All crews are required to have at least one certified person present on the plot at all times.

Field audits—
Hot check. A hot check is an inspection normally done as part of the training process. The inspector is present with crew to document crew performance as they measure plots. The recommended intensity for hot checks is 2 percent of the plots installed.

Cold check. Cold checks are done at regular intervals throughout the field season. The crew that installed the plot is not present at the time of inspection and does not know

when or which plots will be remeasured. The inspector visits the completed plot, evaluates the crew's data collection, and notes corrections where necessary. The recommended intensity for cold checks is 5 percent of the plots installed.

Blind check. A blind check is a complete reinstallation measurement of a previously completed plot. However, the QA crew remeasurement is done without the previously recorded data. The first measurement of the plot is referred to as the field measurement and the second measurement as the QA measurement. The field crews do not know in advance when or which of their plots will be measured by a QA crew. This type of blind measurement provides a direct, unbiased observation of measurement precision from two independent crews. Plots selected for blind checks are chosen to be a representative subsample of all plots measured and are randomly selected. Blind checks are planned to be made within 2 weeks following completion of the field measurement. The recommended intensity for blind checks is 3 percent of the plots installed.

Measurement quality objectives—Each variable collected by FIA is assigned a MQO with desired levels of tolerance for data analyses. The MQOs are documented in the FIA National Field Manual (U.S. Department of Agriculture 2004c). In some instances the MQOs were established as a "best guess" of what experienced field crews should be able to consistently achieve. Tolerances are somewhat arbitrary and were based on the ability of crews to make repeatable measurements or observations within the assigned MQO. Evaluation of field crew performance is accomplished by calculation of the differences between the field crew and QA crew data collected on blind check plots. Results of these calculations are compared to the established MQOs.

In the analysis of blind check data, an observation is within tolerance when the difference between the field crew and QA crew observations does not exceed the assigned tolerance for that variable. For many categorical variables, the tolerance is "no error" allowed, so only observations that are identical are within the tolerance level. Tables A.1–A.3 show the percent of

Table A.1—Results of plot-level blind checks for the South, 2001 to 2004 for available States and years

Variable	MQO requirements	Tolerance	Results Southern FIA region	OBS
	percent		*percent*	*number*
Distance from road	90	No tolerance	81	261
Water on plot	90	No tolerance	90	261
Latitude	99	± 2.3 degrees	100	300
Longitude	99	± 2.3 degrees	88	300
Elevation	99	No tolerance	24	268
Elevation with tolerance	99	± 5 feet	33	268
Public access restrictions	90	No tolerance	86	158
Road access	90	No tolerance	85	158
Trail or roads	90	No tolerance	73	158
Human debris	80	No tolerance	85	261
Distance from agricultural land	90	No tolerance	80	261
Distance from urban land	90	No tolerance	76	261

MQO = measurement quality objecctive; OBS = observations.

Table A.2—Results of condition-level blind checks for the South, 2001 to 2004 for available States and years

Variable	MQO requirements	Tolerance	Results Southern FIA region	OBS
	percent		*percent*	*number*
Owner group	99	No tolerance	99	156
Regeneration status	99	No tolerance	99	162
Regeneration species	99	Nonspecified	99	162
Owner status	99	No tolerance	99	162
Tree density	99	No tolerance	98	162
Owner class	99	No tolerance	97	156
Disturbance 1	99	No tolerance	97	259
Treatment 1	99	No tolerance	96	13
Treatment 2	99	No tolerance	96	3
Physiographic class	80	No tolerance	94	266
Treatment year 1	99	± 1 year	92	13
Forest type (group)	99	Nonspecified	90	162
Forest type	99	No tolerance	85	162
Stand diameter class	99	No tolerance	80	162
Stand age	95	± 10 percent	71	161

MQO = measurement quality objective; OBS = observations.

Table A.3—Results of tree-level blind checks for the South, 2001 to 2004 for available States and years

Variable	MQO requirements	Tolerance	Results Southern FIA region	OBS
	percent		*percent*	*number*
Diameter at breast height	95	± 0.1 /20 in.	87	3,159
Azimuth	90	± 10 degrees	97	3,131
Horizontal distance	90	± 0.1 /1.0 ft.	96	3,131
Species	95	No tolerance	94	3,198
Tree genus	99	No tolerance	98	3,198
Tree status	95	No tolerance	100	3,198
Total length	90	± 10 percent	78	2,980
Actual length	90	± 10 percent	63	180
Compacted crown ratio	80	± 10 percent	81	3,131
Crown class	85	No tolerance	77	3,131
Decay class	90	± 1 class	81	168
Cause of death	80	No tolerance	94	232
Standing dead	99	No tolerance	100	92
Mortality year	70	± 1 year	97	232
Condition	99	No tolerance	100	1,588

MQO = measurement quality objective; OBS = observations.

observations that fell within the program tolerances in the South during 2001–2004. At this time, only the blind check results for plot-level and tree-level variables for the South as a whole can be presented. Too few blind checks were available to permit us to assess results for Tennessee separately from results for the rest of the surveyed region.

Timber Products Inventory

Estimates of timber product output (TPO) and plant residues were obtained from canvasses (questionnaires) sent to all primary wood-using mills in the State. The canvasses are used to determine the types and amount of roundwood (i.e., saw logs, pulpwood, poles, etc.) received by each mill, the county of origin of the wood, the species used, and how the mills dispose of the bark and wood residues produced. The canvasses are conducted every 2 years by personnel from the Tennessee Department of Agriculture, Division of Forestry and the SRS. These data are used to augment FIA's annual inventory of timber removals by providing the product proportions for that segment of removals that is used for products. Individual studies are necessary to track trends and changes in product output levels. Industry surveys conducted in 1999, 2001, and 2003 were used to

determine average annual product output for roundwood and plant byproducts. Total product output, averaged over the survey period 1999–2005, is the sum of the volume of roundwood products from all sources (growing stock and other sources) and the volume of plant byproducts, or the mill residues.

The TPO database can be accessed from the Forest Service SRS FIA website at http:// srsfia2.fs.fed.us.

National Woodland Owner Survey

FIA conducted a questionnaire survey, formally known as the National Woodland Owner Survey (NWOS), to obtain information about the family forest owner group (www.fs.fed.us/woodlandowners). Questionnaires were sent to a sample of private forest landowners in Tennessee during 2002–2004. By design, the sample excluded landowners who own no forest land. A total of 178 survey responses were returned by Tennessee landowners for the 2004 survey between 2002 and 2004 (table A.4). Responses by mail accounted for about 74 percent of all survey responses. The remaining 26 percent were telephone respondents.

Table A.4—National Woodland Owner Survey sample sizes for family forest owners in Tennessee, 2002 to 2004

Response type						
Mail			Telephone			Total
2002	2003	2004	2002	2003	2004	responses
			number			
53	54	25	19	12	15	178

A relative standard of accuracy has been incorporated into the forest survey. This standard satisfies user demands, minimizes human and instrumental sources of error, and keeps costs within prescribed limits. The two primary types of error are measurement error and sampling error.

Measurement Error

There are three elements of measurement error: (1) bias, which is caused by instruments not properly calibrated; (2) compensating, which is caused by instruments of moderate precision; and (3) accidental, which is caused by human error in measuring and compiling. All of these are held to a minimum by a system that incorporates training, check plots, and editing and checking for consistency. Editing checks in the office screen out logical and data entry errors for all plots. It is not possible to determine measurement error statistically, only to hold it to a minimum.

Sampling Error

Sampling error is associated with the natural and expected deviation of the sample from the true population mean.

This deviation is susceptible to a mathematical evaluation of the probability of error. Table B.1 lists the 2004 estimates of land area, and estimates of inventory volume and 1999–2003 components of change on timberland, along with their confidence intervals and sampling errors, expressed in percent. In this case, the confidence interval is the range of values for which there is a two-out-of-three (67 percent) chance that the range includes the true population value obtained from a 100 percent census.

FIA inventories supported by the full complement of sample plots are designed to achieve reliable statistics for the region. Sampling error increases as the area or

Table B.1—Statistical reliability estimates for Tennessee, 2004

Variable	Sample estimate		Confidence interval	Sampling error
				percent
Area (*1,000 acres*)				
Forest land	13,784.0	±	103.4	0.75
Timberland	13,254.0	±	114.0	0.86
Reserved	530.1	±	53.1	10.01
All live (*million trees*)				
Inventory (forest land)	7,779.2	±	115.1	1.48
Inventory (timberland)	7,509.7	±	117.9	1.57
All live (*million cubic feet*)				
Inventory	25,902.2	±	383.4	1.48
Net annual growth	848.9	±	36.0	4.24
Annual removals	615.5	±	48.4	7.86
Annual mortality	38.7	±	1.8	4.73

volume considered decreases in magnitude. Sampling errors and associated confidence intervals are often unacceptably high for small components of the total resource. However, there may be instances where a smaller component does not have a proportionately larger sampling error. This can happen when the post-defined strata are more homogeneous than the larger strata, thereby having a smaller variance. For specific post-defined strata the sampling error is available from online retrievals using the Forest Inventory Data Online (FIDO II) at http://199.128.173.26/fido/mastf/index.html or can be calculated using the following formula. (Note: Sampling errors obtained by this method are only approximations of reliability because this process assumes constant variance across all subdivisions of totals.)

$$SE_s = SE_t \frac{\sqrt{X_t}}{\sqrt{X_s}}$$

where

SE_s = sampling error for subdivision of State total

SE_t = sampling error for State total

X_s = sum of values for the variable of interest (area or volume) for subdivision of State

X_t = total area or volume for State

Precautions

Users are cautioned to be aware of the highly variable accuracy and questionable reliability of small subsets of the data (e.g., volume estimates by county). When summarizing statistics from the FIADB, users should familiarize themselves with the procedures used to compute sampling error, as outlined above.

Species List[a]

Common name	Scientific name[b]	Common name	Scientific name[b]
Softwoods		**Hardwoods (continued)**	
Eastern redcedar	*Juniperus virginiana* L.	Sweetgum	*Liquidambar styraciflua* L.
Shortleaf pine	*Pinus echinata* Mill.	Yellow-poplar	*Liriodendron tulipifera* L.
Table Mt. pine	*P. pungens* Lamb.	Osage-orange	*Maclura pomifera* (Raf.) Schneid.
Eastern white pine	*P. strobus* L.	Cucumbertree	*Magnolia acuminata* L.
Loblolly pine	*P. taeda* L.	Southern magnolia	*M. grandiflora* L.
Virginia pine	*P. virginiana* Mill.	Bigleaf magnolia	*M. macrophylla* Michx.
Baldcypress	*Taxodium distichum* (L.) Rich.	Apple	*Malus spp.* Mill.
Eastern hemlock	*Tsuga canadensis* (L.) Carr.	Chinaberry	*Melia azedarach* L.
		White mulberry	*Morus alba* L.
Hardwoods		Red mulberry	*M. rubra* L.
Boxelder	*Acer negundo* L.	Water tupelo	*Nyssa aquatica* L.
Red maple	*A. rubrum* L.	Blackgum	*N. sylvatica* Marsh.
Silver maple	*A. saccharinum* L.	Swamp tupelo	*N. sylvatica* var. *biflora* (Walt.) Sarg.
Sugar maple	*A. saccharum* Marsh.		
Buckeye	*Aesculus spp.* L.	Eastern hophornbeam	*Ostrya virginiana* (Mill.) K. Koch
Ohio buckeye	*A. glabra* Willd.	Sourwood	*Oxydendrum arboreum* (L.) DC.
Ailanthus	*Ailanthus altissima* (Mill.) Swingle	American sycamore	*Platanus occidentalis* L.
Serviceberry	*Amelanchier spp.* Medic.	Cottonwood	*Populus spp.* L.
Yellow birch	*Betula alleghaniensis* Britton	Black cherry	*Prunus serotina* Ehrh.
River birch	*Betula nigra* L.	White oak	*Quercus alba* L.
American hornbeam	*Carpinus caroliniana* Walt.	Scarlet oak	*Q. coccinea* Muenchh.
Hickory	*Carya spp.* Nutt.	Durand oak	*Q. durandii* Buckl.
Water hickory	*C. aquatica* (Michx. f.) Nutt.	Southern red oak	*Q. falcata* Michx.
Bitternut hickory	*C. cordiformis* (Wangenh.) K. Koch	Cherrybark oak	*Q. falcata* var. *pagodifolia* Ell.
Pignut hickory	*C. glabra* (Mill.) Sweet	Overcup oak	*Q. lyrata* Walt.
Pecan	*C. illinoensis* (Wangenh.) K. Koch	Swamp chestnut oak	*Q. michauxii* Nutt.
Shellbark hickory	*C. laciniosa* (Michx. f.) Loud.	Chinkapin oak	*Q. muehlenbergii* Engelm.
Nutmeg hickory	*C. myristiciformis* (Michx. f.) Nutt.	Water oak	*Q. nigra* L.
Shagbark hickory	*C. ovata* (Mill.) K. Koch	Nuttall oak	*Q. nuttallii* Palmer
Black hickory	*C. texana* Buckl.	Pin oak	*Q. palustris* Muenchh.
Mockernut hickory	*C. tomentosa* (Poir.) Nutt.	Willow oak	*Q. phellos* L.
Allegheny chinkapin	*Castanea pumila* Mill.	Chestnut oak	*Q. prinus* L.
Chinkapin	*Castanopsis* (D. Don) Spach	Northern red oak	*Q. rubra* L.
Catalpa	*Catalpa spp.* Scop.	Shumard oak	*Q. shumardii* Buckl.
Sugarberry	*Celtis laevigata* Willd.	Post oak	*Q. stellata* Wangenh.
Hackberry	*C. occidentalis* L.	Black oak	*Q. velutina* Lam.
Eastern redbud	*Cercis canadensis* L.	Black locust	*Robinia pseudoacacia* L.
Flowering dogwood	*Cornus florida* L.	Willow	*Salix spp.* L.
Hawthorn	*Crataegus spp.* L.	Sassafras	*Sassafras albidum* (Nutt.) Nees
Common persimmon	*Diospyros virginiana* L.	American basswood	*Tilia americana* L.
American beech	*Fagus grandifolia* Ehrh.	White basswood	*T. heterophylla* Vent.
White ash	*Fraxinus americana* L.	Winged elm	*Ulmus alata* Michx.
Pumpkin ash	*F. profunda* (Bush) Bush	American elm	*U. americana* L.
Blue ash	*F. quadrangulata* Michx.	Cedar elm	*U. crassifolia* Nutt.
Waterlocust	*Gleditsia aquatica* Marsh.	Slippery elm	*U. rubra* Muhl.
Honeylocust	*G. triacanthos* L.	September elm	*U. serotina* Sarg.
Kentucky coffeetree	*Gymnocladus dioicus* (L.) K. Koch	Rock elm	*U. thomasii* Sarg.
American holly	*Ilex opaca* Ait.		

[a] Common and scientific names of tree species ≥ 1.0 inch d.b.h. occurring in the FIA sample.
[b] Little (1979).

Tennessee: The Volunteer State

Capital City: Nashville

Location: 36.171 N, 86.784 W

Origin of State's Name: Named after Cherokee Indian villages called "Tanasi"

Nickname: Tennessee has had several nicknames, but the most popular is "The Volunteer State." The nickname originated during the War of 1812 for the volunteer soldiers from Tennessee serving under Gen. Andrew Jackson.

Population: 6,156,719 (2007 estimate)

Largest City: Memphis

Geology:
  Land Area: 41,154 square miles; 34th largest State
  Inland Water: 989 square miles
  Highest Point: Clingmans Dome; 6,643 feet
  Lowest Point: Mississippi River; 182 feet

Border States: Alabama, Arkansas, Georgia, Kentucky, Mississippi, Missouri, North Carolina, Virginia

Constitution: 16th State

Statehood: June 1, 1796

Agriculture: Soybeans, cotton, tobacco, livestock and livestock products, dairy products.

Industry: Chemicals, transportation equipment, rubber, plastics.

Natural Resources: Tennessee's fertile soil, mild climate, huge water systems, and abundant minerals (fluorite, marble, pyrite, zinc, limestone, phosphate rock, coal, small amount of petroleum and natural gas, Ball clay, lignite, sand and gravel, barite) make the State rich in natural resources.

Bird: Mockingbird—According to the Nashville Banner of April 16, 1933, the mockingbird, *Mimus polyglottos*, was selected on April 11, 1933, as State bird of Tennessee in an election conducted by the Tennessee Ornithological Society. It is ashen gray above, with darker, white-edged wings and whitish underparts; its length, inclusive of the long tail, is about 10 inches. One of the finest singers among North American birds, it possesses a melodious song of its own, and is especially noted for its skill in mimicking the songs of other birds.

Tree: Tulip poplar—The tulip poplar was designated as the official State tree of Tennessee by Public Chapter 204 of the Acts of the 1947 General Assembly. The tulip poplar was chosen "because it grows from one end of the State to the other" and "was extensively used by the pioneers of the State to construct houses, barns, and other necessary farm buildings."

Flower: Iris—In 1919, the General Assembly, by Senate Joint Resolution 13, provided that a State flower be chosen by the school children of Tennessee. Accordingly, a vote was taken and the passion flower was chosen. In 1933, however, the Legislature adopted Senate Joint Resolution 53 designating the iris as the "State Flower of Tennessee," but failed to formally rescind the designation of the passion flower as the State flower. To eliminate this confusion, in 1973 the 88th General Assembly, by Chapter 16, designated the passion flower the State wildflower and the iris the State cultivated flower.

Songs: My Homeland, Tennessee; When It's Iris Time in Tennessee; Tennessee Waltz; Rocky Top; The Pride of Tennessee.

Flag: The State flag was designed by LeRoy Reeves of the Third Regiment, Tennessee Infantry, who made the following explanation of his design: the three stars are of pure white, representing the three grand divisions of the State. They are bound together by the endless circle of the blue field, the symbol being three bound together in one—an indissoluble trinity. The large field is crimson. The final blue bar relieves the sameness of the crimson field and prevents the flag from showing too much crimson when hanging limp. The white edgings contrast the other colors.

Seal: In 1796, the Constitution of the State of Tennessee provided for an official Great Seal. A standardized seal was adopted in 1987 by the General Assembly. Although the style of the present seal has changed, the basic elements remain similar to the 1796 provisions.

Motto: The State of Tennessee's motto is "Agriculture and Commerce," taken from the wording used on the State seal. The motto was officially adopted in 1987.

Information courtesy of:
http://www.50states.com
http://wiki.answers.com
http://www.state.tn.us/sos/bluebook
http://www.enchantedlearning.com/usa/states
http://www.netstate.com